MW00779050

Used Cars 101

Used Cars 101:

Humorous Stories and Winning Strategies for Today's Used Car Professional

Steve Hosaflook

Printed in the United States of America.

Hosaflook, Steve

Used Cars 101: humorous stories and winning strategies for today's Used Car Professional- 1st ed.

ISBN   978-0-9826284-0-9

First Edition

This book is dedicated to the men and women working in the Used Car Industry.

For every copy of this book that is sold, a donation of $1 will be made to the Disabled American Veterans (DAV) Charitable Service Trust.

Contents

ACKNOWLEDGMENTS

Thanks to my wife for her constant support, advice, and for being my first reader. Thanks to Bree for being my second reader. Thanks to my family and friends for always listening to my stories. Thanks to my used car family for providing me with a lifetime of memories.

My First Day in the Used Car Business

It was my first day in the used car business, and I was extremely excited. I was scheduled to work from 9 am until 6 pm. I couldn't wait to get started, and I wanted to make a good first impression. So, I arrived at 8 am. No one seemed to notice or care that I was an hour early. This would be my first lesson about the car business. Everyone works long hours. No matter who you are or what your position, you will be working long hours. Unfortunately for me, because I was an hour early and I had zero experience, management felt an appropriate use of my time would be to follow one of our porters while he delivered a vehicle and then shuttle him back to our dealership.

I was introduced to the porter that I would be following in my "chase car." I forget his name and I forget his face, but I remember that he was old. He was VERY OLD. I will refer to him as Old Man Porter. It seemed strange to me that a company would hire a person with bad eye sight and extremely delayed reaction time to be a porter, but what did I know? It was my first day.

I was filled with excitement as the two of us left the dealership in our respective cars. I followed Old Man Porter for about 10 miles. He drove a Nissan Maxima and I was chasing him in a Toyota Camry. It was easy to follow him, because he drove slower than most humans run. He drove slowly, very slowly. However, I didn't care how long it took to get where we were going. I was just excited to be at work. Plus, I didn't even know where we were going or what we would be doing once we arrived. It was my first day.

As we continued on our trip, Old Man Porter began to drive at normal speeds. I remember thinking, "Excellent, we are going to make good time after all." Unfortunately, that was about to change.

We approached a red light in the distance, but Old Man Porter was not stopping. He was not even slowing down. "Stop!!" I helplessly yelled from inside my own car. "Stop!!" He did not stop. I helplessly watched as Old Man Porter rammed a vehicle that was stopped at the red light. **WHAM**!! He slammed right into the rear end of a small Dodge Neon.

I quickly pulled over to the side of the road and exited my car. By this time, Old Man Porter had climbed out of his car and was staggering around in the middle of oncoming traffic. I dodged a few vehicles, grabbed him, and escorted him safely to the side of the road. I then checked on the driver of the Neon. Fortunately, she was not severely injured. I also helped her to the curb and waited for the police and ambulances to arrive.

The police finally arrived, and because Old Man Porter was still very shaken up, I was responsible for answering all of the policeman's questions. Where did we work? Where is your dealer tag? Where is the dealer insurance? Who is a contact person at my store? Where were we going? These were all valid questions. Unfortunately, I didn't know any of the answers. I had not even been working there for an hour yet. The policeman was NOT amused.

Eventually I got enough information out of Old Man Porter that the police could complete their report, and I could drive Old Man Porter back to our dealership. We were supposed to be gone half an hour. We were gone almost three hours. On the drive back to the dealership, I kept replaying the incident over and over in my mind. Right then and there I made a vow to myself. If I was going to work in the car business, I would always be extra careful while driving cars. I wouldn't let accidents stop me from being successful in the car business. There would be no accidents for me. No way.

We eventually made it back to the dealership, where I was yelled at for taking such a long time to deliver one vehicle. However, there was no time to explain where I was or what I had been doing, I was needed elsewhere. This was my second lesson about the car business. If you are going to work in the retail car industry, you will be busy all the time. There will never be enough hours in the day to accomplish all of the things you want to accomplish. It is just the nature of the business.

I was needed in the back lot of the dealership. Our dealership was holding our bi-monthly wholesale auction-an event that required the help of all available employees. Most of the roles in the auction required some type of training or skill. Because I had neither of these things, I was sent to be a driver. I was told to drive the vehicle in front of the auction block and stop. I would then wait until the ringman told me to proceed out of the auction. That seemed simple enough. Drive, stop, and then drive again. I felt confident I could handle those responsibilities. I had no idea what a ringman was, but I assumed I would figure that out later.

I climbed inside my first wholesale vehicle, and two important thoughts ran through my mind. First, it was the middle of August in Georgia, and my vehicle had no air conditioning. It was miserably hot, and I thought I might actually melt. Second, I was reminded of the vow I had just made to myself. I was going to be extra careful while behind the wheel of any vehicle that was owned by our dealership. I would have NO accidents. I would be extremely cautious. I did NOT want to end up like Old Man Porter.

I drove my wholesale car with no air conditioning up to the auction block. I waited, and then a man who was standing in front of the car blowing a whistle tapped my hood and motioned for me to proceed out of the auction. "That must be the ringman," I correctly thought to myself. I proceeded to drive out of the auction. Success.

I was then directed to drive another car through the auction. This procedure continued for another 30 minutes. I was enjoying my time and being extremely cautious. And then it happened. I was following another car into the auction lane, that car stopped, so I pressed the brakes. Nothing happened. I pressed harder and still nothing happened. **WHAM!!** I hit the car in front of me.

The next few minutes were a blur. The vehicle in front pulled through the auction and so did I. Once I parked the vehicle I immediately ran to find the person who was designated to be my mentor. As the auction was proceeding, I had heard many people talking about Old Man Porter getting fired. I was sure that was going to be my destiny too. I was so disappointed in myself. I hadn't even gone one day without an accident. I just knew I was to be fired.

I found my mentor and pleaded my case. In my defense, I exclaimed "The car had virtually no brakes. How was I supposed to stop?" When my mentor and I walked over to the car I was driving, he began to laugh. He said, "This car might be worth $100 on its best day, the small damage on the bumper is the least of its problems. Now get your ass in another car and drive." Then he walked away laughing to himself.

I was stunned. Nothing happened to me. I still had my job. I was thrilled. For the rest of the auction I didn't even mind driving the vehicles that had no air conditioning. My mind eventually started to relax, and I began to pay more attention to what was going on around me. I was in the middle of an automobile auction, and people were doing all of these strange things. Everyone had a cell phone to their ear. People were constantly flipping through books that they were holding in their hands. However, the strangest thing was watching all the people touching and rubbing the cars like they were a genie's lamp. I had no idea why people were doing any of these things. But I didn't care. The excitement of the auction had me hooked. It was an absolutely thrilling experience. This is what I wanted to do. I loved every minute of it.

Six O'clock arrived and I didn't even notice. The dealership closed at 9 PM, and I walked out of the door on my first day at 9:30 PM. I had just worked Thirteen and a half hours. It was a thrilling day and I was exhausted.

It's time for the Used Car Professional to be better.

Not many professions have as bad a reputation as Used Car Managers (UCM) and used car dealers. According to almost every poll taken on the subject, used car professionals are among the least trusted people in the United States. As a person who has worked in the retail automotive industry my entire adult life, this has always been very troubling to me, especially since most of the UCMs and used car buyers that I have met are successful business people who conduct their business in an ethical manner.

Why are used car professionals so disliked and distrusted?

Consumers rely on memories of how the car business operated a long time ago. Forty years ago, the retail car business was totally different than how it exists today. Dealers engaged in all kinds of activities that are now rare occurrences. Forty years ago, odometers were rolled back regularly, titles were forged, and customers were cheated. But those days are long gone. Today's dealerships are regulated by both the government and private sector companies such as Carfax. Yet, the public still dislikes and distrusts us.

Americans have always held the small businessman and the entrepreneur in very high esteem. However, they have often not made the important connection that the local car dealership is a small business. For some reason, they don't recognize the local car dealer as an entrepreneur. Maybe it is because it is difficult to be seen as a "small" business when you are the largest employer in town, which is a common situation in many small towns and communities across America.

The credit crisis of 2008 and the ensuing downturn in the nation's economy have put the American small businessman and the American car dealer directly in the media's spotlight. On a daily basis we hear stories about people being laid off and watch as dealerships struggle to stay open. In 2009 alone, over 2,000 dealerships closed their doors. Many used car professionals have lost their jobs, and the ones that were lucky enough to keep their jobs are finding themselves working longer hours for less pay. Needless to say, these are unprecedented times in our country and in the used car business.

Buying and selling used cars has always been a challenging business, but operating in a deep recession in which credit has virtually disappeared makes a difficult task seem impossible. Fortunately, many used car professionals know how to operate during deep recessions. Most used car professionals have seen hard times before and know how to make money even in the worst of times. These used car professionals are some of the best small business executives in the country.

I believe that many used car professionals are outstanding business people. It is my hope that eventually used car professionals can one day be seen by the American public as the exceptional business people they are. However, for that to happen, the industry needs to improve. As used car professionals, it is our responsibility to improve our industry. It is our responsibility to try and be better.

- We must strive to be better managers.
- We must strive to improve how we service our customers.
- We must strive to improve how we source inventory.
- We must strive to be better salespeople.
- We must strive to be better business people.

The car business is very fast paced. If you are not trying to improve and move forward, you are moving backwards.

The people you meet in the Used Car Business

If I was forced to choose my favorite aspect of the car business, I would quickly choose the people I have met throughout the years. The people employed in the car business are certainly an odd cast of characters. Most of them have larger than life personalities that make business fun and exciting. The relationships that we build with other people in this industry are truly special. These relationships make our industry better and stronger. We are a community made up of individuals, yet we share many things in common. For example:

- Everyone in the used car business works long hours.
- Everyone in the used car business wants the industry to do well.

- Everyone in the used car business wants to sell more cars.
- Everyone in the used car business wants to make more money.
- Everyone in the used car business wants to be happier with their jobs.

In other words, we all want the used car industry to perform better; because the industry consists of people we call colleagues and friends. We want the used car industry to perform better, because we want to do better ourselves.

> *"The secret of joy in work is contained in one word -*
> ***excellence**. To know how to do something well is to*
> *enjoy it."* **Pearl S. Buck**

I have spent my entire adult life working in the retail automotive industry. My first job after college was as a buyer-in-training for CarMax. At CarMax, I was trained by some of the best used car buyers in the country and was quickly given the opportunity to source large volumes of vehicles for some of the largest and best-run dealerships in the world. My years at CarMax were wonderful and provided me with a priceless education about the used car business.

After leaving CarMax, I spent a few years as a UCM at some of the largest franchise stores in the country before I decided to become my own boss. I spent the next five years being a wholesaler and eventually became an independent Dealer Principle.

Over time, my career shifted from being a dealer or a UCM into working for companies that sold to and serviced UCMs. In other words, UCMs were still my customers, but now I provided them with other products and services, not automobiles. It is during this stage of my career that I came to appreciate how stressful and challenging being a UCM truly is.

As a wholesaler, I only did business with 15 to 20 local UCMs. Soon, I was doing business with thousands of UCMs across the country. I would spend every day speaking with UCMs. They talked about every aspect of their business, and I listened carefully. I was tapping into hundreds of years of car experience. I was interacting with every different type of UCM imaginable, many of whom are some of the most successful in the industry.

My personal experiences and the knowledge I have gained from countless conversations with thousands of UCMs and used car buyers comprise the bulk of this book. I also conducted formal interviews with several successful UCMs and wholesalers (see Appendix One), to gain additional insight into our industry. It is my hope that the stories and information contained within these pages provide you with a road map that leads to a happier and more lucrative career in the exciting used car industry.

Section I

INVENTORY MANAGEMENT

Purchasing

One of my favorite sayings from the car business is "the money is made when the car is bought, not when it is sold." As a young "car guy," just learning the ropes, I must have heard that saying a hundred times. Now that I am an older car guy, I use this saying hundreds of times. Why? Because it is one of the truest statements about our industry. If the money is made when the car is purchased, then extra care should be taken to assure that each used car is properly purchased.

Purchasing used vehicles is one of the hardest skills to master in the used car business. The supply and demand structure is constantly changing. The market is constantly in a state of flux. To make things even harder, no two used cars are alike. To be an effective buyer, a person must be both an expert at evaluating the condition of each vehicle and an expert at evaluating the constantly changing marketplace.

Determining the value of a used car is an extremely difficult thing to do. There are no set guidelines to follow, and often it is more of an art than a science. However, there are certain fundamentals and processes that can improve your purchasing decisions.

The purchasing process should be seen as two separate functions: the inspection, and the valuing of the vehicle. These processes should be viewed separately; yet, if a person makes a mistake in either part, it will result in a bad purchase.

Inspections

The first crucial step in learning how to inspect a used car is to DO THE SAME THING EVERY TIME. When appraising a used vehicle, establishing a repeatable pattern is crucial. Follow the old saying "practice makes perfect" and follow the same routine every time. This will help you eliminate mistakes.

"We are what we repeatedly do. Excellence, then, is not an act, but a habit."   **Aristotle**

When buying cars at auctions you sometimes only have seconds to:
- Determine if the vehicle has any paintwork.
- Determine if the vehicle has any frame damage.
- Determine if the vehicle is mechanically sound.
- Calculate the market demand for that specific vehicle.
- Determine how much money you should pay for the vehicle.

A good used car buyer can perform all of these functions within seconds. How can they perform all of these functions so quickly? Simple; they follow the same routine on each vehicle they appraise and buy. Having an established pattern is crucial whether you are buying 20 cars an hour at an auction or a single car through your appraisal process.

Get your own routine and stick with it. Do the same thing every time.

It's important to establish a pattern that works for you, one that you are comfortable with. I always start examining a vehicle at the driver's side fender. I then proceed to the hood, and then continue moving clockwise around the vehicle, looking for signs of paintwork and frame damage, until I return to my starting point. I start at the driver's fender because that is where the VIN plate is located.

I do this because I will NOT buy a vehicle across the auction block if I have not personally verified the year of the vehicle with the VIN plate. This habit stems from purchasing a 1998 Mercury Mountaineer that turned out to be a 1997. The markings on the windshield from both the dealer and the auction read 1998. The auction failed to arbitrate the vehicle for me and I lost $1500 in a matter of seconds. Did that hurt? You bet it did. When buying used cars, we all make mistakes. The important thing is to learn from those mistakes. I learned my lesson, and I never made that mistake again.

Following the same routine will help you reduce the number of reconditioning issues you overlook and perform a more thorough inspection. You can't accurately establish a used car's value if you can't appraise the vehicle properly.

Being a good car inspector is similar to being a good detective.

You must learn to think like a detective during the inspection process. Your job is to find the clues that are hidden on and in the vehicle. These clues will tell you if the car has had a rough life or a nice life. These clues will tell you if the car was well maintained or not. These clues will tell you if it's a vehicle you want or one you want to avoid.

I use every technique at my disposal when I am inspecting a car. I have several things I am looking for, but my two main concerns are evaluating the car for prior paintwork and any possible frame damage. I focus on these two issues because they are the two parts of the vehicle's appearance that will cause the most damage to a vehicle's value.

Frame damage is obviously more severe, but paintwork is more common. Also, it is rare that a vehicle's frame would be damaged if the car has no paintwork. In other words, by eliminating the possibility of paintwork we can also eliminate the possibility of frame damage. Paintwork is also important because it serves as a major warning sign. Noticing a car or truck has been painted tells the inspector to pay very close attention. Paintwork usually means the vehicle has been in some type of accident. It could have been a severe collision or a harmless incident with a grocery cart. The problem is, at first glance after the car has been repaired, it can be hard to know just how severe the accident was. The severity of the accident can usually be determined through careful testing of more evidence. To perform this testing we will use two very basic instruments. We will use our eyes and our hands.

There are two different tests that help you search for post-factory paintwork. They are the *feel test* and the *sight test.* In other words, use your hands and eyes. Cars that have been painted in the factory *feel* and *look* different than cars that have been painted at a dealership or body shop. A factory paintjob is always going to be better than a vehicle painted at your local body shop or dealership. Why? Because local dealerships and body shops can't make the same investment in creating state-of-the-art painting environments as major car manufacturers can. Are there good auto body men in your local town or city? Sure. But, are they as good as a multi-million dollar, precise paint machine operating in a dust-free clean room environment? No way.

Feel Test

I constantly touch any vehicle that I am inspecting. Using your sense of feel can be a very powerful tool in establishing whether or not a vehicle has been in an accident.

You should be touching every edge on every panel on every vehicle you inspect. You should constantly be feeling for evidence of rough edges. Rough edges are an easy sign to recognize, and usually means that the panel has been painted. You also want to feel each panel for tape lines that have resulted from the vehicle being painted.

Sight Test

Keeping a consistent inspection routine will help train your eyes to instantly spot problems with a vehicle's appearance. Things that you should be looking for on every vehicle you inspect include:

- Wrench marks that are left on bolts that have been turned. These marks are most common on the bolts holding the fenders and the core support.
- Fish eyes within the paint.
- Junk and other particles found in the paintwork.
- Sand lines.
- Tape lines.

If all else fails, use modern technology.

If you want a quicker, but more expensive way to detect paintwork, you may want to purchase a paint elcometer. Recently, elcometers have become increasingly popular. Rarely do I meet a highline buyer who doesn't use one. Further, they are extremely valuable during rain or snow storms, when visibility is limited. They are highly accurate and very easy to use. They are more expensive than using your eyes and hands, but not as costly as buying a used car with a complete paintjob and frame damage.

Frame Damage

Frame damage... the words strike fear into the hearts of used car buyers everywhere. Frame damage is definitely not good. Frame damage usually occurs when a vehicle has been involved in an accident so severe that the structural integrity of the frame itself is damaged. Having the car's structure compromised can lead to a serious value reduction and can even pose a safety risk. Fortunately, this kind of impact is very difficult to hide, making our jobs as appraisers much easier. There are several places on a vehicle to look for evidence of frame damage. To avoid purchasing a car with frame damage, spend some time examining the core support and the frame rails of the vehicle.

The core support is critical to a car's integrity. A front end collision that is severe enough will damage the core support. When you are investigating the structural integrity of the core support, look for any bolts that have been turned and altered on the core support. Wrench marks left on the bolts of the core support are usually a sign the fender or the actual core support itself has been removed from the vehicle.

Even though the frame rails are located underneath the vehicle, they should not be neglected in your inspection routine. Usually the frame of a vehicle gets altered if it has been in a severe collision. Fortunately for us, when a vehicle is put on a frame machine there will be *evidence* left on the frame rails. The frame machine has to "clamp" the car's railings. This clamping process leaves a mark that is easily detected, making our inspection job much easier.

Are clamp marks on the frame rail definitive evidence of frame damage? Yes, most of the time, but not always.

I have appraised a few cars that had clamp marks and no paintwork or frame damage. This situation can occur when a body man or a mechanic places the car on a frame machine simply to align the vehicle.

Even though it is *possible* to have clamp marks without frame damage, it isn't very likely. Clamp marks usually mean the vehicle was in a serious accident and the vehicle's frame has been compromised. In most cases, it is better to be safe than sorry, and you should treat any vehicle with clamp marks as having frame damage.

Often Overlooked Items

There are several other aspects of the vehicle's appearance that affect its appraisal value. All of these items can be easily seen and should not be overlooked when determining both reconditioning costs and the vehicle's value. These objects include: tires, windshields, and rust.

Tires

When appraising a car, take the time to carefully examine the vehicle's tires. Tire replacement is one of the largest reconditioning expenses at any dealership. Nobody wants to replace tires if they don't have to, so give them a thorough inspection. First, check to see if all the tires are the same brand. Then, check to see if the tires have an adequate amount of tread. Check to see if the tires have any puncture or nail holes. Lastly, rub your hand on the inside of each tire to assure the tire is not cupped due to a bad alignment. You are looking for the tire's tread to have a consistent depth on both the inside and outside of the tire. Certain vehicles have tires that can easily cost over $200 a piece, so take the time to examine each tire.

Windshield

Take the time to check the windshield and the back glass for cracks and stars. Cracks usually mean the windshield will need to be replaced. But what about a star in the windshield? Can it be fixed or does the entire panel of glass need to be replaced? This complicated question can easily be solved by using a standard American Quarter. Lay the quarter over the star. Does the quarter completely cover the star? If so, then the star can probably be filled for a small fee (usually around $35-$50). If the star spreads beyond the quarter, it usually indicates the windshield will need to be replaced. This method is not 100% accurate but it is very close.

Rust

Looking for rust, especially if you live in a cold climate or near the ocean, is another important step that needs to be part of your appraisal process. While you are examining the frame rails, take a look at the rest of the "under belly" of the vehicle. Examine the brakes and the strut towers carefully; these are two common areas for rust to form

These smaller items, such as: tires, rust and cracks in the windshield can quickly increase your reconditioning costs. However, by staying consistent with your routine and diligent in your examination you will become increasingly better at finding these issues.

Test Drive

The final piece of the inspection process is the test drive. As UCMs and used car buyers, there will be plenty of vehicles that we purchase before we have an opportunity to test drive. Most of these vehicles will be purchased from the auctions. It is nearly impossible to test drive every car you **might** buy at an auction, which is why most people only test drive the vehicles they have actually purchased.

Most auctions offer a post sale frame and mechanical inspection for a modest fee. These post sale inspections can be a great benefit to the used car buyer. The auction inspectors do a thorough job and will automatically arbitrate vehicles that have severe problems. These types of post sale inspections are even more helpful for dealers who travel long distances to attend auctions. For dealerships located far away from an auction, it is difficult to even get a car home and inspected within the arbitration guidelines. Further, the post sale inspection eliminates the possibility that the vehicle will have to be shipped twice. If you are attending a sale that is far away from your dealership, I highly recommend using the auction's post sale inspections.

As a general rule, I would use the post sale mechanical inspection if the vehicle was beyond the manufacturer's warranty. For all of the vehicles that were still under warranty, I would simply take them on a test drive.

Test driving vehicles at car auctions is not always the easiest and safest thing to do. All auctions have rules regarding test drives. Some auctions have a designated area where test drives can be performed. I always take advantage of these areas. Some auctions do not have a designated area, making it more difficult to test out the vehicle in a safe manner. Safety should always be your highest priority when driving a vehicle at any auction. If the auction you are attending offers a test drive track, please take advantage of it.

Appraisals performed at the dealership should always include a test drive. We should always take advantage of the opportunity to really test out a vehicle. When test driving a car, the route you take will greatly affect the amount of information you can obtain while on the test drive. Pick a route that has a significant amount of straight road. This is where you can test the vehicle's acceleration, transmission, and braking abilities. Also, make sure you include some curves and turns in your test drive routine. This will allow you to adequately test the vehicle's steering and the vehicle's CV joints and boots.

However, the most important thing to do while on a test drive is...

Turn down the radio and listen.

When test driving any vehicle, always listen carefully. If you listen closely, the vehicle will tell you all you need to know about its mechanical condition.   If you don't know what is causing a certain noise, ask one of your mechanics. It is also a good idea to ride along with some of your mechanics when they do their test drives. Mechanics have become experts at listening to vehicles, and they are usually very happy to share their extensive knowledge with you.

Things to keep in mind when performing inspections

- Get your own routine and stick with it. Do the same thing every time.
- Being a good car inspector is similar to being a good detective.
- Focus on finding paintwork and frame damage.
- Frame damage is more severe, but paintwork is more common.
- Use your hands and eyes.
- Elcometers are very effective.
- Don't overlook: tires, windshields, and rust.
- Post sale inspections can save you time and money, especially at sales that are long distances from your dealership.
- When test driving a vehicle, turn down the radio and listen.

Valuation

"When you are selling a used car, it is worth what someone else will pay YOU for it. When you are buying a used car, it is worth what YOU will pay THEM for it." **Steve Hosaflook**

Valuation is extremely tricky to determine in the used car business. Learning how to properly value a used car or truck is a difficult task to master. If you try to pay too little, you won't have enough quality merchandise on your lot, and you will lose sales. If you pay too much, you will go broke. When valuing used cars, the stakes are high.

- Used car valuation is part science and part art.
- Used car valuation is ALWAYS a matter of opinion.
- Used car valuation involves other people.
- Used car valuation can immediately change.

Used car valuation is part science and part art.

First let's deal with the **science** part. Let's talk about the statistical analysis and the information that is published by the leading used car data providers. There are several different companies that provide historical sales information on the prices of used cars. You can get this information online or in book form. These data providers aggregate large amounts of data to determine their prices. They monitor and report the results of hundreds of thousands of vehicles that are bought and sold at wholesale auctions.

This information is extremely important when determining a price for a used vehicle. Because the used car market is constantly changing, vehicles can have enormous price swings from week to week. Receiving current information from one of the reporting services is critical in keeping up with the quickly changing used car market. In other words, make sure you are carrying the latest market information. Don't go to the auction with a book that is a month old.

Now for the **art** part of valuation. Pricing information is used differently by different people, even in the same dealership. A typical scenario would be: the used car buyer might only reference the Black Book. The Finance & Insurance (F&I) manager probably only uses the NADA Guide because that is how he communicates to the broader banking community to get a loan approved. The person who does the new car pricing might only use Kelley Blue Book. And the shocking part is that each one of these people will probably come up with a completely different valuation for the same used car, depending on which company's information they are using. Sometimes these differences can be quite significant.

Even if you find a group of people who use the same reporting service (i.e. Black Book, NADA, etc...), they won't use the information in the same way. What's more, they will use the information differently on every car. Some buyers will not pay more than *clean book* for any vehicle. Some buyers are very strict users of the adds and deducts. Some buyers pay much more than *clean book,* for the right kind of car. Some cars are worth way less than *rough book.* A buyer who will pay "out of the book" for one type of car will only pay *average* for another make and model with the same mileage and condition.

In other words, there are hundreds of used car buyers using different sources of information in a hundred different ways for thousands of different vehicles.

Valuation is ALWAYS a matter of opinion.

It is impossible to keep track of all the different ways that people determine the value of a used car. It is impossible to know exactly how someone else determines value. Further, it is impossible just to get everyone looking at the same statistical information. Given all of this, how is it possible to know what a car is really worth?

Do you want to know precisely what a used car is worth? That is a very easy and simple thing to determine. It is very easy to establish the value for most things. If you take away nothing else from this book, remember this:

When you are selling a used car, it is worth what someone else will pay YOU for it. When you are buying a used car, it is worth what YOU will pay THEM for it.

In other words, value is in the eye of the person writing the check. This is a very easy concept, yet the majority of UCMs do not understand it. **What YOU paid for something is irrelevant. It is only worth what someone will pay YOU for it.** Thoroughly understanding this concept is one of the major differences between the elite UCMs and an average UCM. The professional knows that previous pricing information is irrelevant. They leave emotion aside and deal strictly with what someone will pay for a vehicle.

I can't tell you if the car you just bought was worth *clean book* or not. I can't tell you if the high mileage vehicle you just appraised is worth *rough book*. However, there is one way to find out what it is worth. **Pick up the phone and call someone who will buy it and ask them.**

A tiny bit about the Used Car Business

Calling a Car

Having the ability to properly "call a car" is extremely important in the used car business.

The process that used car professionals use to describe a vehicle to other professionals is commonly referred to as "calling a car." This condensed and strange language used by car people to communicate seems like gibberish to most outsiders. Every industry and profession uses their own form of communication and their own slang. Calling a car is our industry's version of shorthand. Calling a car is not a science. Calling a car is an art form. Calling a car is painting a picture of a vehicle with words. Your words and descriptions have to paint a mental image in your customer's mind for the call to be effective. This ritual, used by car dealers to describe and purchase inventory, is one of the most fascinating aspects of the used car business. Right or wrong, this is how we communicate. It is how we buy and sell vehicles. Just like other forms of communication, there are rules, and there are people who are better at calling cars than others.

The ability to quickly and concisely describe a vehicle in a pleasant manner is certainly a skill that can be learned. Further, it is a skill that we can all improve today.

First, make all of your "calls" fit the same kind of pattern. Be consistent with your descriptions. Don't mention miles early sometimes and last other times. Keep it consistent. Consistency paints a clearer image in the listener's mind and it allows you to add selling emotion when the time is appropriate.

I follow the same pattern every time. Calling or describing a vehicle to me is second nature. It is something I could do in my sleep. Because I have followed the same pattern for so many years, my customers have gotten used to my pattern. This allows me to communicate the necessary information and add selling emphasis where it is needed.

Everyone has a different sales technique when they are calling cars. I usually mention the best part about the car last. I want the best selling item to be the last thing in my customer's mind before they offer me a price.

The most important thing when calling a car to your customer is to BE HONEST. Always be honest. Is the car a sled? If so, communicate that. Your customer is going to know it is a sled eventually. Call a sled a sled, and call a gorgeous car a gorgeous car. You DO NOT want to be labeled as the boy who cried wolf. This can be death in the car business. If you oversell a crappy car, your customer will remember. This makes it nearly impossible to get your customers to pay more for the cars that are truly nice and truly deserve a premium paid.

Is it possible to know everything about a particular used car? Of course it isn't. But, we can strive to know as much as we can about a car and describe that to your customer. In the long run, honesty is a better policy. If you hold back information or tell "white lies" about your cars, eventually your customers will stop buying from you. You will also spend most of your day dealing with returns and the problems that arise from miscalled cars.

To make your life simpler and more profitable, tell the truth, the whole truth and nothing but the truth.

Receiving a call from someone trying to sell a vehicle that hasn't learned how to properly *call a car* can be a painful experience. Often you have to ask them several questions and still don't receive a good mental picture of the vehicle they are trying to describe.

When you are receiving a call on a car, there are only a few things to remember. Always ask questions if you are unsure of something and write the information down. As a used car buyer I would receive almost 100 calls a day, and I would put buy figures on most of the vehicles that were called to me. With this type of volume, it became virtually impossible to remember all of the specifics about each car. Writing down the information helps eliminate any confusion that may occur regarding the condition or the features of the vehicle.

Used car valuation involves other people.

Because used car prices are constantly changing, it is imperative that used car buyers consistently maintain the pulse of the market. This is impossible to do by yourself, so it is important to be in constant contact with other used car professionals that you trust.

It is crucial to have trustworthy people you can use as a sounding board for car prices. We all have our favorite people who we like to call to get their opinion about different cars. Some buyers are experts in highline cars, some buyers are experts in a certain make or model, others are experts about cars with very high miles, etc. These are the people you should be calling to get their feedback about the current marketplace.

These are also the people you will be calling to help you determine a vehicle's value. Remember, a used car is only worth what someone will pay you for it. Therefore, if you really want to know what a car is worth, try to sell it.

Valuation can immediately change.

The value of a used car is constantly changing. Normally, the value is depreciating. Sometimes a car's value can dramatically change in a very short period of time. This can be caused by the condition of the car itself, for example, the engine gets destroyed. Or, it could be caused by changes in the condition of the overall market.

It is difficult for people to change their opinion about a car's value, and admit when they have made a mistake. However, when a dramatic change in the value of your vehicle happens, the quicker you adjust your thinking to reflect the vehicle's new value, the better off you will be.

Everyone remembers what they were doing on the tragic day of September 11, 2001. Everyone who was in the car business at the time will never forget the dramatic effect this horrible incident had on our country, but also on our industry. The month that followed September 11th was one of the lightest volume months in the history of the car business. The country was still in shock, and no one was buying cars. Thanks to the manufacturers dropping their interest rates to 0.0%, sales began to pick up in mid October and remained strong for a few years. But, for about a month, the entire used car market seized up and stopped working.

The used car market was in a state of panic. Cars lost huge amounts of money virtually overnight. A car that was worth $10,000 on September 10th was worth $8,500 on September 12th, and $7500 by September 14th. Valuations were constantly plummeting. Anyone who was holding inventory at that time lost money.

I was wholesaling, and fortunately I was carrying very little inventory, which spared me from losing too much money. But, many people were not that lucky. Another wholesaler that I worked with had just purchased 8, like-new, Cadillacs from a Cadillac dealer. All of the vehicles were frontline vehicles with low miles. He purchased the vehicles on September 10th and had verbal commitments for most of the cars. By September 12th, all of the commitments were rescinded, and he was stuck holding 8 unsold front-line Cadillacs.

It was difficult to even keep up with how fast these cars began to depreciate. Each new week brought a new Black Book. Each new Black Book brought terrible news. The book value and the market value for these cars were sinking faster than a leaky boat. Time was of the essence. Every day was precious in trying to recoup as much money as possible.

The market had changed overnight. The Cadillacs were no longer worth what they were worth only a few days earlier. The valuations had immediately changed. Fortunately, the wholesaler quickly adjusted his thinking to this new reality. He eventually sold all of the vehicles. Unfortunately, he lost a considerable amount of money. However, the damage would have been much worse if he had waited. His losses would have been much more severe if he hadn't quickly adjusted to the new price level that the market dictated. The bottom line is this, valuations can change immediately and when they do, you need to adjust your thinking to reflect the vehicle's new value immediately. The longer you wait, the more money you will eventually lose.

Learning how to inspect and value used cars is one of the hardest skills to develop in the used car business. Once you develop these skills, you still have to put your knowledge to use and purchase inventory. Most inventories are sourced at the **auction** or through the dealership's **trade-in** procedure.

Auctions

I love car auctions. Don't you?

For many years, I made my living at car auctions. To me, a car auction is one of the most exciting places in the world. I'm sure there are many out there who feel the same way. Fortunately for us, car auctions happen five days a week, giving us plenty of opportunities to make large sums of money and to lose large sums of money. I love car auctions, don't you?

Sourcing vehicles at auctions has become the lifeblood of any used car department. Rarely will the vehicles that are traded in at your dealership be adequate enough to fill your lot. Either the trade-ins will be too rough, have too many miles, or just be the wrong mix of vehicles. We have no control over what kind of inventory we take in on trade, so proper auction management is essential in any successful used car operation.

Where does good auction management come from? It comes from excellent preparation.

"Chance favors only the prepared mind." **Louis Pasteur**

Excellent preparation is the key to making money at any auction.

First, get to the auction as early as possible. For some, this will mean arriving a day before the sale, for others this will mean arriving as early as possible on the day of the sale. Arriving early is even more important if you are a wholesaler. Wholesalers usually need extra time to call potential buyers before making their purchases. Arriving early gives a person plenty of time to inspect the cars they are interested in and take note of any damage.

Typically, you start with your "needs list." Which vehicles do you need to buy? Do you need a specific vehicle for a particular customer? Start by pulling the run list and search for the vehicles you need. Once you have compiled your list, you can inspect the vehicles you selected to assure their cosmetic and mechanical quality.

Doing your auction preparation early also allows you the opportunity to gather extensive pricing information using various Internet sources. We are all familiar with the Manheim Auction online database of prices. This is a wonderful source of historical pricing information and should be used to complement and verify your thinking as often as possible. When you are trying to calculate used car valuations, there is no better starting place than a list of what vehicles actually sold for in recent auctions. This information is extremely valuable.

Once your research is complete, now comes the tough part, deciding what you will pay for a vehicle.

How do used car professionals determine what they will pay for a used car? There are as many techniques as there are car buyers. Everyone has their own style and their own way of measuring value. Remember, valuing used cars is part science and part art. Some buyers will only use the Black Book. Some buyers use NADA or Kelley Blue Book. Some use the adds, some don't. Some use the mileage deducts; some just use a lower designation instead of the deducts. There are countless different ways of determining value.

A used car has no set value. This fact makes it very difficult to source and manage a used car inventory. However, if a buyer knows how much a vehicle retails for, he can determine an appropriate price to pay for any used car. Accurate pricing information allows past sales information to guide future purchasing decisions. This kind of information gives a used car buyer an immense amount of knowledge and power.

I only used one method to determine what I should pay for a vehicle at an auction. I worked backwards from what I could sell the car for. Simple, yet complicated. What I could sell a vehicle for was the only number that mattered to me when buying a vehicle. Whether I was wholesaling or running a retail lot, I always worked backwards from a selling number.

I have worked at non-haggle, fixed-price dealerships and haggle dealerships where the selling prices can vary greatly. The job of the buyer is certainly much more difficult in a haggle environment. In these cases, you will usually work backwards from a range. For example, your sales data will show that you can sell a certain vehicle between $13,000 and $14,000 instead of a specific number.

Working backwards from a single selling price is much easier at a non-haggle, fixed-price dealership. The flagship of non-haggle is CarMax, The Auto Superstore. CarMax's one price approach revolutionized the used car business. People point to different factors that make CarMax successful. In my opinion, the genius behind the CarMax system of selling cars is their ability to work backwards from a firm retail selling price. It is the piece of the puzzle that makes everything else work so well.

However you determine how much you will pay for a car, come up with a top amount you will pay. Then, **write it down**. Always keep the top dollar amount you will pay for a vehicle in a place where it is easily accessible. Auctions can become confusing. You might lose the auctioneer's rhythm or notice something on the vehicle that would change its value, or you might get into a bidding war with another dealer. If you have your pricing information written down, it will take some of the emotions out of the bidding process and save you from making simple mistakes.

Once you have a top dollar amount, *stick to it.* Do not pay over your top amount. This can be a difficult thing to do in the heat-of-the-moment at an auction. Sometimes we get wrapped up in the excitement and overpay for a vehicle. A *good* buyer knows how to buy a car; a *great* buyer knows how to NOT buy a car. A great buyer knows when to **walk away**. If you are unsure of the price you should pay, **walk away**. If you are unsure of the vehicle's quality, **walk away**. If you are unsure about anything,

walk away. Opportunities are easier to make up than losses. Besides, there will be another auction tomorrow and the following day. There will always be another opportunity to buy a vehicle. There is no need to over pay.

Auctions will often move very fast. Proper prep work will help you avoid costly mistakes that happen when a person is rushed. Excellent preparation leads to fewer mistakes and higher profit.

Things to keep in mind about auction preparation

- Arrive Early, Arrive Early, Arrive Early.
- Determine a top dollar amount you will pay for each vehicle.
- Do NOT pay above this top dollar amount.
- Opportunities are easier to make up than losses.
- A good buyer knows how to buy a car; a great buyer knows when to walk away.

A tiny bit about the Used Car Business

Auction Food

Car auctions offer something for everyone to enjoy. Some people love the thrill of buying a car across the auction block. Some people love selling a car for more money than they expected. I love both of those things. But, sometimes things don't work out too well at an auction. Sometimes, the market goes against you. Sometimes, you even lose money at an auction. But, there is one thing that is always consistent at car auctions. There is one thing that can always be counted on to be enjoyable, THE FOOD. I love auction food. I love everything about it: the grease, the portions, the breakfasts, the lunches, everything.

I have always been a "cup of coffee for breakfast" kind of person, so it's difficult for me to do a quality breakfast analysis. Nevertheless, if you are a lover of "country breakfasts," the car auction breakfast is something you will truly enjoy. Auctions offer a wide selection of options for breakfast. These options include: biscuits and gravy, eggs, sausage, and bacon. Sometimes the eggs come out of a box and the food has been sitting under a heat lamp for too long. But most of the time, I find the breakfasts that are served at most auctions to be homemade and excellent.

Auction breakfasts are good, but lunch is where the real quality food is served. Some of my favorite dishes can be found at many car auctions. Auctions don't serve fast food junk; they serve labor intensive, home-cooked meals like meatloaf or turkey and stuffing. Auctions also serve fantastic grill food, such as hamburgers, hot dogs, and french fries.

A typical auction burger.

Out of all the auctions across the country, my favorite place to have lunch is the Manheim auction in Lancaster, PA. This auction is nestled in the heart of Amish country and offers some of the best "home-cooked" meals I have ever tasted.

Breakfast at the auction.

We all have our favorite dishes from our favorite auctions.
Vote for your favorite auction food at
www.UsedCarVoice.com.

When purchasing inventory, mistakes will be made

"It is by presence of mind in untried emergencies that the native metal of a man is tested."
James Russell Lowell, "Abraham Lincoln"

When purchasing used cars, you will make mistakes. We all make mistakes. If you are the world's best used car buyer, you will still make several mistakes throughout your career. Mistakes will happen during your trade-in process and at auctions. However, due to the speed of the auctions, you are more likely to make a mistake at the auction than you will at your own dealership. Even though mistakes are commonplace, they can dramatically affect your ability to perform your job. What happens when you make a mistake at the auction? Do you dwell on your mistake? Does it affect the rest of your time at the auction? Do you beat yourself up about it for days? Or do you shrug off mistakes before they can affect your future actions?

It is very easy to get down on yourself when you make a mistake at an auction. But, these kinds of self defeating thoughts will only cause you to miss out on other opportunities at the auction, or at worst, distract you even further, leading to more mistakes. Quickly refocusing your attention after a mistake is a difficult thing to do, but it is necessary.

One of the single best days I ever had as a wholesaler began with a mistake. I was attending the Adesa Charlotte auction. I was primarily in attendance because of their Honda Finance sale. In my opinion, at the time, it was the best auction in the Southeast to source Honda Products. I had arrived at the auction the day before the sale, walked the entire presale inventory, and made extensive notes. At the time, I had several buyers in Atlanta that were willing to pay very strong money for Hondas and Acuras. I also had a good sense of the price level that the vehicles would bring at the auction. I felt very confident that I would be able to purchase many high margin vehicles. I felt very confident that it was going to be a money-making day at the auction.

The 4th car of the auction was an Acura CL in wonderful condition and with very low miles. I had established that I would pay up to $15,000 for this car, because I had a buyer for the vehicle committed at $16,000.

The auctioneer started the bidding at $14,000, and I hit the bid. The auctioneer received no more bids, slammed the hammer down, and in a matter of seconds I had bought my first car of the day. I was extremely happy. I quickly calculated in my head that after transportation expenses, I had just made around $1,600. I thought to myself "I love this business; this is going to be a great day."

Two minutes into the auction and I was already up $1,600.

I had some time before the next vehicle I was interested in buying was available for sale. So, I quickly walked to the pre-sale area to get another look at the gorgeous $14,000 Acura I had just purchased. When I arrived, I noticed she was a pretty car, not a scratch on the paint and exceptionally detailed. I was getting more and more excited about the car until I noticed something very troubling. The car had a manual transmission!! My heart sank immediately! I completely missed it. Normally Acuras don't come with a manual transmission, but this CL did. Also, the stick in the CL looks similar to an automatic shifter at a quick glance. But these were all just excuses. The fact was I had been careless. I had made a very serious mistake. I had just LOST $1500 to $2,000.

Two minutes into the auction and I was already down $1,500 to $2,000.

I no longer loved this business. I cursed and cursed. I cursed the dreaded car business. I cursed myself for being so careless. I cursed the Acura engineers. I cursed until I got it out of my system... or for approximately five to ten minutes.

Earlier in my career I might have let this mistake affect me for the rest of the day, but not this day. I regained my composure and tried to focus on the rest of the auction. The mistake was in the past and there was nothing I could do to stop it from happening. All I could do was move forward. I reminded myself that profitability lies in the road ahead. Besides, I had done a lot of homework and preparation for this sale. Before the sale started, I felt confident that this would be a profitable sale for me and I started replaying the reasons why I felt this way inside my head. This sale had excellent inventory. I had customers who were expecting cars and had given me very strong buy figures. I remembered that I had many other opportunities to buy cars that would make money. I began to relax. I began to regain my confidence.

I focused even harder. I thoroughly inspected each vehicle as it rolled into the auction, even if I had already inspected the car several times. I wanted to be correct on every decision for the rest of the day, and I was. I was right 13 more times. In total, I bought 14 cars that day. I bought 13 that made money and one that lost money. In the end, the CL didn't cost me as much as I thought. It was still in very nice condition with extremely low miles. After all of my expenses, I only lost $1200 on the CL.

This was one of my most financially rewarding days ever as a wholesaler, I ended up selling the other 13 vehicles for very nice margins, and my customers were very happy with the condition of their vehicles.

"Good judgment comes from experience. Experience comes from bad judgment." **Unknown**

The bottom line is this- we all make mistakes. It is how we recover from our mistakes that truly defines who we are and how well we will perform in the used car business.

The Trade-in Process

Besides sourcing vehicles at the auctions, we can also source vehicles through our dealership's trade-in process. Used Car Managers should pay more money for vehicles that come through their trade-in process than they do for vehicles sourced through the auction or through wholesalers. Paying more for a vehicle that is being traded, compared to the same vehicle at the auction, is always a good idea. When you buy a vehicle through your trade-in process, you are earning your customer's trust and their business.

Why not pay more for a trade-in vehicle? Why help another dealership by paying strong money for their car at an auction? Help your customer instead. If you have to reward someone, wouldn't you rather reward your current or potential customer, rather than your competition?

Appraisers and buyers can also perform more thorough inspections with trade-in vehicles than they can with auction vehicles. If the vehicle is being traded, an appraiser can thoroughly test-drive the car and even have a mechanic inspect it. These procedures should make you more comfortable with estimating reconditioning costs and allow you to pay customers more money for their trade-ins.

Vehicles purchased at the auction will be charged a buy fee and usually a transportation fee. Trade-in vehicles do not have these costs associated with them, which allows the UCM to pay even more for a customer's vehicle.

When you buy a car at an auction, it is a very cut and dried transaction. The car is put up for sale, people bid, the hammer slams down, and you sign some paperwork. The entire process is quick and virtually free of any customer interaction. Because the trade-in procedure involves a customer, it is much more complicated and intimate than the auction buying process. The customer will be the one who ultimately has to agree with the trade-in price to complete the transaction. Successful UCMs understand this and take steps to properly establish a customer's expectations.

Setting the customer's expectations is one of the most important aspects of any trade-in process. Some UCMs or buyers do not speak to the customer before the appraisal. This can be a big missed opportunity. The trade-in process gives the UCM a chance to build rapport with the customer and provides an opportunity to adjust the customer's expectations if it is needed.

Spending time with your customer before the appraisal gives you an excellent opportunity to explain your appraisal process to your potential customer. I have found these interactions to be very productive. Customers do not like to be kept in the dark. It is difficult for customers to accept prices that just "magically" appear. It is important to explain to them what you are looking for in the appraisal process and how you will establish a value for their vehicle.

My pre-appraisal "pitch" was very standard for every customer I met. I explained that I would be looking for: paintwork, frame damage, and mechanical soundness during my appraisal and test drive. I also explained how these factors can negatively affect a vehicle's value. With regards to how I was going to value this specific car, I simply explained I would be offering replacement value for their car. In other words, if I had to go into the marketplace today and source that exact car, how much would it cost me? I would also explain that there are numerous sources (Manheim online, NADA, Black Book, etc) that compile this information, making my offer relatively easy to verify. This simple explanation helps instill trust with the customer.

Meeting the customer before the appraisal is also an excellent opportunity to gather marketing information. This type of information gathering can be accomplished by interviewing the customer or by having the customer fill out a questionnaire about their car before the appraisal. Appraisal forms can be complicated or very basic. Whichever kind you decide to use, I encourage you to use some type of appraisal form.

What should be on an appraisal form? The best appraisal worksheets I have seen include many questions for the customer to answer. Questions like...

- Did you buy the vehicle new or used?
- Do you have complete service records?
- How often do you change your oil?
- When was the last time your vehicle was serviced?
- What was your vehicle last serviced for?
- Do you have the title for the vehicle?

The appraisal form is also an excellent place to ask market research questions, such as...

- How did you hear about us?
- How often do you trade in your vehicle?

- How far have you traveled to be with us today?
- Have any of your family and friends purchased a vehicle from us?

These marketing questions will give you better insight into your customer's wants and needs. They will also help you better define your customer demographics. Having this kind of marketing information will be invaluable when it comes time to advertise or during any customer service follow ups.

You should also put information limiting your liability on your appraisal form. For example, an appraisal form should contain language that lets the customer know that your dealership is not responsible for items left in the car during an appraisal.

Each appraisal form should have a sentence or two that warns an appraiser of any dangers they might incur during an appraisal.

Such as, **please notify the appraiser if there are any potentially harmful items in your vehicle or any known conditions your vehicle might have that could affect the appraisal or injure the appraiser. Thanks**.

If your appraisal form does not include verbiage similar to this statement, **please add it as soon as possible.**

In my career I have encountered the following things while doing appraisals...

- Loaded guns.
- Angry dogs.
- Snakes.

- Vehicles with virtually no working brakes.
- A hive of fire ants.
- Vehicles with terrible steering problems.

Needless to say, a little warning can go a long way. Don't make your appraiser find out the hard way that your customer's vehicle is a death trap. This type of statement can also help eliminate other costly customer service claims.

Having a warning statement would have been helpful to me several times during my career. For example, one particular incident quickly comes to mind. It was near closing time, and I was getting ready to go home. I had one appraiser out on a test drive, and once he was done, I would be finished for the night. He had been gone a long time, and I began to wonder what was taking him so long. When he finally made it back to my office it was obvious that he was very upset.

He was appraising a Jeep Grand Cherokee and everything was going fine until the test drive. He went on to explain that during the test drive, the hood of the Jeep flew open and smashed the Customer's windshield well beyond repair. My appraiser was still very shaken up by the incident and was definitely not in any condition to tell the customer that we just did a severe amount of damage to his vehicle.

I immediately called my head porter to find a loaner vehicle for the customer, preferably a Grand Cherokee. I then went to speak to the customer. Needless to say, he was not very happy when he saw the condition of his vehicle. He was so upset that he no longer wanted to buy a vehicle from us. His exact words were something like "I will never buy a car from you guys; wait till you hear from my attorney."

Those are not words you want to hear 5 minutes before closing time. At that moment, my porter pulled up in a Grand Cherokee that the customer could use as a loaner vehicle. This seemed to slightly ease the customer's rage. I explained to him that "unfortunately accidents happen, and we would make this situation right." I told him that we would immediately fix the hood and windshield free of charge or he was welcome to take the Jeep to a body shop of his choice, and we would pay the bill. Neither of these options seemed very appealing to him. He told me that he was going home, and he would call me in the morning with his decision. I eventually left the dealership three hours after the customer's appraisal began.

Fortunately, the customer LOVED the Grand Cherokee that he was given as a loaner. When he called me first thing the next morning, I was expecting to hear his wrath. Instead, he pleasantly told me that he loved the vehicle he was driving, and if we could make the trade-in numbers work; he would purchase the Grand Cherokee that he was currently driving.

Did I pay-up for the Grand Cherokee with the busted hood and windshield? You bet I did. I paid $1500 more than it was worth. The customer had me and my dealership over a barrel. He had all the leverage, and I had none. So, I paid him way too much for his trade-in, but at least we gained a car deal. In the end, we turned a very angry potential customer into a relatively happy customer.

I sat down with the appraiser to explain the importance of properly closing the hood during an appraisal. He was extremely apologetic. He said he had learned his lesson, but he continuously swore to me that he had in fact closed the hood. He apologized more and we eventually resumed our normal daily activities. The next day, I received some interesting news from the mechanic who was servicing the damaged trade-in. He showed me how the hood latch was defective. There were even pieces of twine left in the latch from where the customer had been tying down the hood. In other words, the customer knew that the vehicle's hood would fly open. He knew his vehicle was going to be severally damaged. He knew my appraiser would be in an accident and could possibly be severely injured. Yet, he said nothing. Not only did he jeopardize the life of one of my appraisers, he also received a terrific price for his trade-in.

This incident is why I always place the sentence... **Please notify the appraiser if there are any potentially harmful items in your vehicle or any known conditions your vehicle might have that could affect the appraisal or injure the appraiser. Thanks**.

Then, I ask all customers to sign their names acknowledging this statement. I have found that most people will treat something more honestly and seriously when asked to sign it. By asking for a signature, it establishes this as something important that should be taken seriously. This will normally cause them to disclose any information they have been trying to hide.

Trade-in appraisals are exactly like buying vehicles at the auction or from wholesalers, except for the customer interaction aspect. All of these customer-centered procedures can increase the number of vehicles that you are able to source through your trade-in process, thus increasing your sales and adding to the profitability of your dealership.

The people you meet in the Used Car Business

A car is a very personal possession. As used car professionals, we sometimes forget this because we are constantly buying, selling, and driving different vehicles. Further, as purchasing agents, we try to remain emotionally neutral when appraising and purchasing any vehicle. But, for most Americans, their car is a sanctuary. It can be a home away from home. It is an extension of them and they take great pride in their choice of vehicle. I was reminded of this when I met a customer to do an appraisal on his 3 year old, low mileage, pearl white Lexus GS 300.

At the time I was a huge fan of this make and model. I was excited to do an appraisal on this vehicle because I knew I would pay very strong money for the car and it would be an excellent seller on my lot, especially because it was pearl white. But, once I met the customer my enthusiasm quickly disappeared. I remember seeing him from across the showroom. He had his head in his hands and looked like he had been crying. I introduced myself and told him I would be appraising his vehicle.

"It's not worth much," He said. "Well, it was, but now it isn't. Here are the keys, go look for yourself."

I grabbed his keys and headed out to the customer parking lot to find his vehicle. I was expecting the vehicle to be sitting on the back of a tow truck. From the customer's expression, I assumed his very nice Lexus had been in a horrible accident. And that's when I saw it.

It was easy to spot in the parking lot. It was probably easy to spot from space. It was painted **NEON ORANGE**- the color of orange that is reserved only for hunting season and Tennessee football games. It was bright and it was UGLY. What's more, the orange paint wasn't even applied well. It was a terrible paintjob. There was overspray everywhere. Parts of the vehicle, like the underside of the hood, were still pearl white. It was one of the worst paintjobs I had ever seen. The car was hideous, and I was speechless.

I had no idea what to appraise the vehicle for. At the time, pearl white, low mileage GS300s were selling at the auctions for around $25,000. However, this was no ordinary GS 300. Yes, the car had great miles, but it was one of the ugliest vehicles I had ever seen. I had to know more about this vehicle, so I went back inside to speak with the customer.

"I told you" he said. I asked him what happened and he told me a very sad story. He loved his car. He had bought it new and babied it every day of its life. "I always get the oil changed at exactly 3 thousand miles, but I was busy this time, so I asked my wife to get the oil changed for me." Unfortunately, this gentleman was in the process of getting a divorce from his wife. I'm not sure if their divorce had been hostile **before** the oil change, but I can guarantee it became hostile **after** the oil change.

I don't know who was to blame for the divorce, but his wife certainly got the best of him with regards to his car. She didn't take his car to get an oil change. She took it to the world's worst body shop and had it painted the ugliest color I had ever seen on a vehicle. She destroyed the vehicle's value, and she destroyed his spirit. This guy was devastated. He was even more devastated when I offered him only $10,000 for his car. However, he sold it to us on the spot. He told me that he physically couldn't look at the vehicle anymore. It hurt him too much. This experience reminded me of two very important pieces of information.

- People love their cars.
- Hell hath no fury like a woman scorned.

What to Buy and How Many to Buy

Purchasing inventory is one of the hardest skills to master in the used car business. Once you master it, you still have to determine the right cars to buy and how many to buy. These two elements are essential to increasing the profitability of your used car department. Unfortunately, these two things can be very difficult to determine.

When sourcing used cars, the goal is not to buy the cheapest car. The goal is to buy the car that has the greatest percentage of selling with the highest profit margin.

First, let's tackle what to buy.

What to Buy

There are thousands of different options of used cars you can purchase for resell. There are hundreds of different makes and models to choose from, with each make and model having different option packages. Also, each vehicle's price and its corresponding demand will be affected by its mileage. With so many options, how does a used car buyer determine which vehicles to buy?

The easy answer is to *"buy what you sell."* However, it is slightly more complicated than that. *Buying what you sell* means that you will have to perform some statistical analysis on historical information instead of merely relying on your "gut instinct." Some UCMs rely solely on their gut instincts when buying used cars. You watch them buy cars at the auction, and they tend to buy a little bit of everything. They have no method for determining what they will purchase. If a car looks and *feels* right, they buy it.

One of my favorite "gut instinct" buyers was the UCM of a very successful import franchise in Atlanta. He seemed to have a good feel for what kind of inventory would do well at his store. His used inventory was slightly cheaper and had more miles than most of his competitors, because his dealership's typical used car customer had subprime credit. Fortunately, his dealership had a wonderful subprime financing program. Therefore, most of the vehicles on his lot were purchased because they worked well within these financing programs. After working at the dealership for many years, he just knew which cars would work in these programs and which vehicles would not. Unfortunately for the dealership, that UCM quit and was replaced by another "gut instinct" buyer. The new buyer didn't have the same feel for the inventory as the previous UCM. Furthermore, the dealership had very poor sales reports available to the new UCM because the previous UCM kept most of this information in his head.

I met the new UCM and talked to him about his situation while waiting for cars to come through the chutes at an auction. He pointed to a red Corvette that was only 2 years old with very low miles that was about ready to run across the block. "I'm buying that Vette" he said. "Wow, is it nice?" I asked. At this point, I felt the Vette might have extensive paintwork or something else wrong with it in order for it to be cheap enough to sell on the UCM's lot. "It's perfect" he replied.

"Isn't that going to be the most expensive car on your lot?" I asked him. "It won't be on my lot for long. It's a red Corvette in spring time. My salespeople sell a ton of cars, and most of them are miley and not very nice. If they can sell that crap, they can sell a red Corvette." He replied.

His "gut instinct" told him that his salespeople could easily sell a gorgeous red Corvette. He then proceeded to purchase the Vette, which sat on his lot for 90 days until he took it back to the auction, where he eventually sold it for a significant loss.

If his salespeople were so good, why couldn't they sell this red Corvette? What he didn't understand was that his sales staff sold so well because they had the proper inventory to sell. Having the right inventory makes every used car sales person seem like a superstar.

Instead of using my feelings or my "gut instinct" I prefer hard analysis of historical sales numbers to determine what kind of inventory is appropriate to buy. I don't totally dismiss an experienced buyer's instinct, but I prefer cold hard numbers. My personal buying style is probably 90% analysis and 10% instinct.

Which numbers do you need to analyze? This is a tough question to answer because it depends on your dealership. In general, you need to look at sales information across different time frames. You want to see how your sales are trending for the past year, the past 90 days, and the past month. You want to determine your top 10 or 20 sellers.

You need to see how your sales break down among the different: makes and models, price points, mileage parameters, and any other metric you think is important. Once you have assembled all of this information you will be able to answer very important questions about your inventory.

- Do you do well with cars under $15,000?
- How about $10,000?
- Do you do well with full size trucks with over 100,000 miles that sell for under $10,000?
- Do you do poorly with full size cars that sell for over $20,000?
- What is your quickest seller?
- What is your slowest seller?
- What is your highest margin seller?
- What is your lowest margin seller?
- What is your top seller?

It must be noted at this point, that your historical sales data will be influenced by all of your past purchasing decisions. In other words, if you have never purchased a full size 4X4 truck with over 100,000 miles, you will not know if you can sell one or not. Or, if you have 50 used cars in inventory and 40 of them are Hondas, you will obviously sell more Hondas than anything else.

Once you have analyzed all of the data, you will know exactly which types of cars your dealership sells quickly and which ones sell for the biggest margins. Then simply go buy those vehicles. In other words, *buy what you sell.*

How Many to Buy

When managing a used car inventory, knowing **how many** vehicles to purchase is also extremely important. Because vehicles are always depreciating, if you purchase too many, you will have higher carrying costs and higher wholesale losses. If you purchase too few, you will lose potential sales. There are several factors that go into determining how many vehicles you should be sourcing for your dealership. These include:

- The size of your dealership.
- How many vehicles you sell.
- How long it takes to recondition your vehicles.
- Any one-time event that may affect the number of vehicles that are needed to be sourced.
- The time of the year.

The size of your dealership.

The size of your dealership will always affect the number of vehicles that need to be purchased. If the area designated to hold your used inventory is only 20 spaces, then your purchasing options will be limited to only 20 vehicles. However, most used car lots are designed to hold more vehicles than is appropriate for them to have in inventory.

How many vehicles do you sell?

To determine how many vehicles to purchase, you should begin with how many vehicles you typically sell in a month. Let's assume you sell 40 used cars a month. What's more, you sell these 40 cars in a very precise manner; you sell exactly 10 vehicles a week. In this simplified example, your purchasing plan would consist of 10 vehicles a week. This also assumes each vehicle is frontline ready and will need no time for reconditioning.

How long does it take to recondition your vehicles?

As a UCM or a used car buyer, you should always know how long it takes vehicles to be reconditioned at your dealership. Since vehicles are constantly depreciating, it is important to monitor your reconditioning time. If it takes too long for your vehicles to reach your frontline, you will lose a considerable amount of money in depreciation. The amount of reconditioning time is key when determining how many vehicles need to be purchased for your dealership. Using the 40 cars a month example from above, let's also assume that it takes each of your vehicles one week to complete its reconditioning process. Then you would know that the cars you buy this week will not hit your front lot for 7 days and adjust your purchasing levels accordingly.

Any one-time events that may affect your purchasing levels.

You should always be aware of any special circumstances that will affect the number of vehicles you need to purchase. For example, let's assume a large amount of your technicians will be going on vacation around the 4th of July, which is also a large volume time for your dealership. In this case, you would want to increase your purchases a few weeks before the 4th, so that all of the vehicles can make it through your reconditioning process before the techs go on vacation. Another example is if you are planning a large tent event, you may need to purchase more vehicles strictly for the increase in traffic related to that event. The recent Cash for Clunkers program is an excellent example of how onetime events can affect your purchasing volume.

The time of year.

Seasonal changes can be one of the easiest concepts in the used car business to understand, and yet they cost dealerships money, year after year. You should buy more vehicles during the spring and summer months and fewer vehicles during the fall and winter months. This is simply based on historical sales trends. It never fails to amaze me how many dealerships are surprised when summer ends and the vehicles on their lots and the ones they take to the auctions begin to rapidly depreciate. This cycle repeats every year, yet it still surprises people.

One of the best examples of this seasonality concept is how well inexpensive cars do during tax season. This is also very easy to predict because the sales pattern repeats itself every year. Each spring, cars that can be priced under $10,000 actually appreciate because the demand for them is so high. The demand is high because consumers are getting their tax refunds and using that money to buy cars. This happens every year at the same time. Yet, every year in late December, these vehicles can be sourced for less money than they will be worth in just a few short weeks.

Every year, when I was a UCM, buyer, or wholesaler, in the middle of December I would start sourcing inexpensive "tax season" vehicles. Every year, it seemed that no other buyer was even remotely interested in buying these kinds of vehicles- probably because sales are always slow during the winter months. I would buy as many of these vehicles as I could and hold them until mid to late January. Since they are cheaper, their lower prices mean they experience virtually no depreciation during this time period. Then, I would simply send the same cars back through the auction when people would be fighting each other to purchase inexpensive cars. This seasonality effect happens every year. A savvy UCM can take full advantage of the cyclical nature of the car industry and buy when prices are low and sell when prices are high.

Things to keep in mind about purchasing

- The money is made when the car is bought, not when it is sold.
- The supply and demand structure for used cars is constantly changing. The market is always in a state of flux.
- When inspecting a used car, do the same thing every time.
- Being a good car inspector is similar to being a good detective.
- When inspecting a car, use both your hands and your eyes.
- During a test drive, turn down the radio.
- Used car valuation is part science and part art.
- When you are selling a used car, it is worth what someone else will pay YOU for it.
- When you are buying someone else's used car, it is worth what YOU will pay THEM for it.
- Used car valuation is ALWAYS a matter of opinion.
- Used car valuation involves other people.
- Used car valuation can immediately change.
- Excellent preparation is the key to making money at any auction.
- Once you have determined a top dollar amount, stick to it.
- When attending an auction, Arrive Early, Arrive Early, Arrive Early.
- If you are purchasing used car inventory, you will make mistakes.
- Trade-ins are an excellent source of inventory.

- The appraisal form is an excellent place to ask market research questions.
- Knowing what to buy and how many to buy is as important as knowing how much to pay.
- Buy what you sell.
- If you don't know exactly what you sell the best, figure it out.
- Buy as many as you sell and closely monitor your reconditioning time.
- The car business is seasonal.

Reconditioning Used Vehicles

Once you have purchased inventory, you need to recondition it.

Whether you are a wholesaler or a used car manager, how you recondition your used cars will have a major effect on your business. The reconditioning process is one of your biggest expenses and a source of some of your biggest headaches. Whether your recon work is performed in-house or you use vendors, managing this process can be challenging and time consuming.

The reconditioning process is important because it costs you both **time** and **money**, which will dramatically affect your profit margins.

Two of the largest expenses in used car departments are depreciation and reconditioning. Every dealership faces constant depreciation risk with their used car inventory. The longer the dealership owns a vehicle, the higher the depreciation expense. Thus, most used car managers focus significant energy on reducing the amount of time their dealership owns a vehicle. This goal can be met by reducing the time required for reconditioning (work-in-process), the time available for sale, or both. Further complicating this process, of course, dealerships must not compromise quality standards simply to speed up their reconditioning processes.

The reconditioning process is important because it costs you both **time** and **money**.

Save Time

From the moment a used vehicle is purchased, time becomes one of the dealership's biggest threats to that unit's profitability. In addition to concerns about a vehicle's depreciation, other outside forces establish their own time constraints upon the dealership. For example, each vehicle purchased at a wholesale auction is subject to the arbitration rules for that particular auction. Arbitration standards vary across the spectrum of auctions, but a limit of seven days from the time of purchase is the standard for arbitrating frame damage and severe mechanical issues. This timeframe can be even more demanding if the vehicle requires several days to be transported.

One way to reduce your reconditioning cycle time is to exam how your cars *flow* through your reconditioning process. It is important to not only have a set routine but to follow the routine. Reconditioning work usually breaks down into different departments. How much time each car spends in the various departments should be constantly monitored and improved. In other words, if cars should only take one day to make it through your detail process and they are taking three days, there is some problem in the detail department that needs to be addressed. It is also important to have a routine in place that quickly and efficiently transfers vehicles from one department to the next once the work has been completed and approved.

Efficiently moving a vehicle from one recon department to the next can be performed in several ways. A transition can be smoothly accomplished by something as simple as the finishing department physically moving the vehicle to the next department once it is ready. Some dealerships keep paperwork in the vehicle during the recon process that lists what services have been performed and who has approved the work. This type of documentation helps cars move quickly through your recon process. There are even software programs available that can monitor how efficiently vehicles move between departments within the reconditioning process. Whichever technique you use, as long as it helps move your vehicles through reconditioning faster, your dealership will be more profitable.

Save Money

You can save money in your reconditioning process by making more informed and better decisions. When making reconditioning decisions, there will be some easy decisions. Each dealership or wholesaler has a certain quality standard they will not go below. Many dealerships post their inspection and quality standards for the world to see. This will make many of your reconditioning decisions very cut and dried. For example, if you state that all cars will have a certain amount of tread, then tires that fall below that threshold must be replaced. On the other hand, there are numerous reconditioning decisions that are not black and white.

Approving a high reconditioning bill can be a complicated process. If you planned for the reconditioning costs appropriately before you purchased the vehicle, you should be able to recondition it without affecting your margins. Unfortunately, many expenses only show themselves once a vehicle has been purchased.

Sometimes the reconditioning bill slowly accelerates, which can be very dangerous. These situations are very tricky and remind me of the story about the frog and the boiling water. The story states that if a frog is placed into a pot of boiling water, it will immediately jump out and save itself. But... if the frog is placed into a pot of relatively cool water the frog will allow the water to be slowly heated, not noticing the rising temperature, the frog will eventually die. Reconditioning bills that rise incrementally place the UCM in the same dangerous position as the frog.

The problem in these situations is *sunk cost*. We often make decisions because we have a certain amount of expenses already *sunk* into the car and we feel our best hope is to "retail out" of the situation. However, this path of thinking often leads to very costly mistakes.

We all know how the scenario plays out: once the car has been reconditioned and placed on the front lot, something else goes wrong with the vehicle. Maybe the electrical system causes a problem on a test drive; maybe the engine starts leaking oil. Whatever the cause, your reconditioning bill unexpectedly goes up. Now the UCM has a decision to make, does he sink more money into reconditioning or does he cut his losses?

This is where the UCM really needs to study past sales data. Is this a car the dealership sells very well or is it a slow selling vehicle? This type of information will help determine how much more money should be spent reconditioning the vehicle. Sometimes it is advisable to take a small margin or even lose a small amount and try to retail out of the vehicle. However, it has been my experience that once a used vehicle has a certain number of mechanical problems, it usually continues having problems. In other words, once a lemon, always a lemon. Sometimes it is best to sell a vehicle for a loss, just to get rid of it.

Vendor Management

You can also save money in your reconditioning process by having better relationships with your vendors.

Vendor relationships are difficult to maintain. Reconditioning vendors come in all shapes and sizes. Some are skilled craftsmen; others are talentless hacks. In the used car business, having a dependable reconditioning technician who performs quality work is truly a treasure. In most dealerships, the UCM is responsible for the physical appearance as well as the reconditioning costs of a used vehicle. Some dealerships have a recon manager who oversees the reconditioning process, but most of these responsibilities still fall under the control of the UCM. Because of this, we spend a lot of time meeting with our current vendors and other vendors who are interested in performing work for us.

I enjoy having vendors try to convince me that I should use their services. Whether they pull dents or merely detail a car, I am always open to finding new talent within the reconditioning world. I find that many vendors are unprofessional and perform sub-standard work. This makes the credible vendors easily stand out from the rest.

One person in particular stands out as being very effective at getting my attention and earning my business. He was a dent technician named Gary who presented himself at the dealership and waited patiently until he could speak to me (UCM) and my General Sales Manager.

He politely asked if we were happy with our current PDR vendor. Many UCMs have used the same PDR vendor for many years, and will never change. Our dealership was not in that kind of position. Quite frankly, I was slightly unhappy with my current PDR technician, but not so unhappy that I was actively looking for a new vendor. However, Gary won us over with his professionalism and his craftsmanship.

Gary presented us with a portfolio of his work. He also included letters of praise from many of his retail and wholesale customers. Finally, he offered to remove the dents from some of our vehicles to prove his abilities. I never turn down free work, so I found a few older vehicles that were destined for the wholesale auction and let Gary proceed. Needless to say, Gary did a wonderful job and immediately earned the chance to work on some saleable vehicles.

A very curious thing happened; having Gary work on some of our saleable cars immediately improved the price and performance of our current PDR technician. Soon, we were getting excellent work and lower prices out of both PDR vendors. Eventually, Gary ended up becoming our sole PDR vendor when the other vendor moved out of state, and he continued providing excellent work throughout my tenure at the dealership. This experience left me a firm believer in the importance of creating competition among your reconditioning vendors.

Vendors should respond to competition by improving. You should stop using the ones that don't improve. Creating competition between vendors can be a big win for your dealership. Your reconditioning money is valuable, and you should create an atmosphere that motivates vendors to provide their best service at the lowest price possible. In other words, make your vendors earn their jobs.

Are your vendors earning your business every day?

Things to keep in mind about reconditioning

- The reconditioning process is important because it costs you both **time** and **money**.
- Time is one of the dealership's biggest threats to every unit's profitability.
- How much time each car spends in the various reconditioning departments should be constantly monitored and improved upon.
- You can save money in your reconditioning process by making more informed and better decisions.
- Beware of letting sunk costs affect your decisions. Remember the frog in the boiling water.
- You can also save money in your reconditioning process by having better relationships with your vendors.
- Make your vendors earn your business.

Merchandising

"Advertising moves people toward goods; merchandising moves goods toward people."

Morris Hite

A dealer's saleable inventory is his life blood. The cars available in your saleable inventory will be one of the biggest factors in how successful you are as a used car manager. One of the most important variables in effective inventory management is how your saleable vehicles are merchandised.

Merchandising and organizing the front lot of a dealership is a daily and weekly practice among car professionals. Each dealership has their own merchandising philosophy that they follow. Some dealerships prefer to organize their inventory along make and model lines. Others choose to organize by price. There are countless ways a front lot can be organized. The specifics of how you merchandise are not as important as actually having a merchandising plan and sticking to it.

I have found that grouping similar types of cars together is an excellent starting point. Trucks go with other trucks, mid size cars are parked next to other midsized cars, etc.... Once this basic organization is established, then it is important to create a sense of uniqueness for each vehicle within the groupings. Used car buyers want the vehicle they are purchasing to be special. They want to feel like their vehicle is unique. Therefore, careful consideration should be taken to separate vehicles that are too similar. In other words, don't park a 2008 green Honda Accord directly next to another 2008 green Honda Accord. When the customer sees 2 or 3 vehicles that are nearly identical sitting next to each other, the customer will naturally lose a sense of urgency. They will lose the sense that their vehicle is unique. This is the opposite of how new vehicles should be merchandised, but that is another book.

However you choose to merchandise your vehicles, the two most important things to keep in mind are, keep it **clean** and keep the lines **straight**.

We all know that having a clean inventory is a priority. If it wasn't important, we wouldn't spend so much money getting vehicles detailed and looking "show room ready." This is a very simple concept, but a very important one. Special care should be taken to assure that your entire saleable inventory is presented in the best manner possible. We all know this, yet sometimes we let our guard down and our inventory presentation slips. For example, we might let a vehicle into our showroom that isn't properly detailed. Keeping your inventory in top shape requires constant focus.

Customers appreciate inventory that is merchandised properly. Having an organized front lot containing perfectly straight rows of cars demonstrates a dealership's level of professionalism. Keeping your inventory aligned properly is also a very challenging task. Cars are constantly being taken for test drives and moved all over the lot. It is virtually impossible to get sales consultants and others to repark their vehicles appropriately. It is frustrating when you begin the day with a perfectly straight row of cars and by 4 PM, that same row is completely crooked.

There are many techniques used to straighten inventory. Some dealerships use lasers, others use the "eyeball" method. This is where someone will simply look at a group of cars and determine if they are straight. However, this method is not very effective.

The simplest and best technique I have encountered requires 2 traffic cones, 2 sticks or broom handles, and some string. Place the broom handles in the cones and connect the two cones with the string. Then, simply pull the vehicles up until they touch the string. This inexpensive method will create straight lines and is simple for porters and salesmen to follow.

Merchandising also includes how you brand each of your vehicles. This can be an important advertising tool for your dealership. Do you put a decal of your dealership's name on each of your vehicles? Do you have a custom drive out tag and tag frame that advertises your name and image? If not, steps should be taken to change this situation.

I had the pleasure of working with one of the major distributers of these kinds of products, Guardian Auto Products, headquartered in Atlanta Georgia, servicing the entire United States. During my tenure at Guardian, I spent a lot of time discussing this type of advertising with hundreds of car dealers. Nearly all of them told me that this kind of post sale branding and advertising has worked extremely well for their dealerships. When a customer is driving and spots another vehicle that came from your dealership, it helps reinforce their purchase decision. Further, this type of advertising will help draw new customers to your location.

Balloons, hanging tags, streamers, etc...

Each dealership has a different philosophy on the use of balloons and other items to decorate cars on the front lot. Some dealerships use these different items to draw attention to their dealership. Obviously, the type of dealership you have will help determine your merchandising style. For example "buy here/ pay here" lots should look differently than a Ferrari dealership. Whatever kind of dealership you manage, spend some time thinking about different ways to merchandise your cars and your front lot. There are several different tools and methods you can choose from that will fit the type of look you are trying to achieve. The proper merchandising style, implemented properly, will go a long way in driving customer traffic to your dealership and to your saleable vehicles.

A tiny bit about the Used Car Business

Attending an auction and merchandising your lot are excellent ways to get exercise.

Do you want to be happier at work and make more money? **Walk more**.

Walking is great exercise and we all know that exercise is good for us. Yet, many of us in the used car profession avoid it. Our idea of exercise is driving to the store to pick up a pack of cigarettes to wash down the fast food meal we just finished.

Walk more. Walking will improve both your health and your wallet. The answers you seek as a UCM are not behind your desk. They are outside. Your inventory is outside. Your customers are outside. Walking your inventory enables you to not only spot cosmetic damage on your vehicles; it helps give you a different perspective of your dealership. It enables you to see your dealership through the eyes of your customer. Being more active with your inventory will be highly beneficial to your bottom line and your health.

I am constantly amazed at the number of diet plans available on the market today. There are diets that require you to eat only protein. There are diets that require you to eat only vegetables. There are diets that require you to eat virtually no vegetables. There are diets where you eat only soup; others where you drink only smoothies. There is the Atkins diet, the South Beach diet, and the list goes on and on.

This seems like over kill to me. I prefer K.I.S.S.- Keep It Simple Stupid.

If a person wants to lose weight, they need to eat less and exercise more. However, knowing what to do is simple; it is the implementation of any plan that is difficult. For example, we know that eating less fast food would help us lose weight and be healthier, yet we rely on fast food when we are busy or when we spend all day in the car. Once again, the knowing part is easy; it is the implementation that is difficult.

> *"Lack of activity destroys the good condition of every human being, while movement and methodical physical exercise save it and preserve it."* **Plato**

We know that walking is both good for our health and good for our inventory management, but it will also sharpen your mental abilities. The better physical condition you are in, the sharper your mind will be. Human beings are one organism. We are comprised of both our bodies and our minds. The two cannot be separated. When our bodies become run down, so do our emotions and our mental abilities. Therefore, if you want your mind to work better, take better care of your body.

Walking is an easy way to put more exercise into your daily routine. As used car professionals we are constantly walking. Whether it is at an auction or at our own dealership, we are always on our feet. You should embrace this. Many UCMs wear a pedometer on their belts so they can know precisely how many steps they took each day. It is fascinating to see how much a used car professional will walk compared to a cubicle-bound employee.

Recently there has been a lot of information released about the health benefits of walking 10,000 steps a day. How far is 10,000 steps anyway? The average person's stride is approximately 2.5 feet long. That means it takes just over 2,000 steps to walk one mile, and 10,000 steps is approximately 5 miles.

To review, walking your lot and walking the auction is:

- Great exercise.
- Good for inventory management.
- Good for your mind.
- Helpful in gaining a customer's perspective.

Section II
PEOPLE MANAGEMENT

People Management

> *"The best soldier does not attack. The superior fighter succeeds without violence. The greatest conqueror wins without a struggle. The most successful manager leads without dictating. This is called intelligent non aggressiveness. This is called mastery of men."* **Lao-Tsu, Tao the King**

The success of your dealership will depend on your employees. If you want your dealership to succeed, hire and train good employees. If you want well-trained employees, hire and train good managers. Having a good management team is the key to unlocking the hidden potential of your employees. This, however, is very challenging. Effectively managing other people is a difficult task, it requires a certain attitude and specific abilities. It requires its own unique skill set.

Just because people perform tasks well, it does not necessarily follow that they can also manage others who are performing the same tasks. In other words, if a person is great at selling cars, it does not necessarily mean they will be good at managing other people who are selling cars.

Dealerships fall victim to the same logic pitfalls as most other corporations when they promote people to management. We want to reward the employees who have performed well for us. We want to reward employees who show tremendous ability in performing their assigned task, whether that task is sales or accounting. Unfortunately, we often feel that the best way to reward these employees is to promote them to management positions that oversee the same tasks they were previously performing.

But, is this truly rewarding the employee? Different people are motivated by different things. Some are motivated by money. Others want to make a difference and accomplish goals. Each individual brings his or her own life experiences and goals to the table. Therefore, each individual likes to be rewarded in different ways.

When thinking about rewarding an employee with a promotion, three main questions should be addressed:

- Is a promotion the best form of a reward that you can give the employee?
- In the long run, is the promotion going to return the best outcome for the organization?
- Does the employee have the temperament and ability to be an effective manager?

Is a promotion the best form of a reward that you can give the employee?

It is always a good idea to reward employees who achieve excellence. People want to get more out of a job than simply a paycheck. Recognition is one of the main things people hope to achieve in their work. In this way, we are all very much alike. We all like to hear the words "good job."

"We are all motivated by a keen desire for praise, and the better a man is, the more he is inspired to glory."   **Cicero**

Presenting awards and giving recognition packs a bigger punch if the recognition is timely and public. The tried and true management saying is "Praise in Public." It is very important to praise publicly, but the timeliness of the praise is just as important. If you want to celebrate someone's success, why wait? Celebrate NOW. When you have employees who deserve praise, give them the recognition they deserve as publicly and as quickly as possible.

When rewarding employees, it is important to remember that everyone is different. This is especially true when the reward is a promotion to a management position that supervises other employees. Quite frankly, not everyone thinks of this as a reward. Some people would prefer to remain at their current positions- jobs they enjoy and make lots of money doing.

There are other ways to reward employees besides giving them titles and new responsibilities. They could earn more vacation time, allowing them to spend more time with their families. They could receive more money. They could receive a demo to drive. They could have access to the best parking spots. There are numerous ways to reward and recognize your best employees.

In car dealerships, the position of sales manager is usually given to the person with the most sales. This new title usually comes with a pay raise and added responsibilities. Before you automatically promote your best sales person to the position of sales manager, you should ask yourself, in the long run, is the promotion going to return the best outcome for the organization?

Here is a typical promotion scenario. One top-notch salesman emerges from the pack of sales people in a dealership. We will call him John Q Salesman. John is every General Manager's dream employee. He is a selling machine. John is extremely focused on selling cars. He comes in early, and he stays late. He spends all of his free time working the phones to set a few more appointments for the day. What's more, he is an excellent closer. John closes better than anyone the dealership has seen in 10 years.

Eventually a sales manager position opens up. The dealership wants to reward John for all of his hard work, and his sales numbers make him the obvious choice. John is extremely excited about his promotion and his new responsibilities. However, he is slightly concerned about his lack of people management experience. John has never supervised anyone before, and now he will be in charge of an eight person team.

John's new title is "Sales Manager" which is misleading because John's new task is actually to manage the **people** who are selling the vehicles. However, because of his new title, he concludes that his new task should be managing his team's sales. John knows he is a fantastic salesman, so he naturally wants to use his ability to help his team.

Unfortunately, this means he is constantly interrupting his team members while they are interacting with their customers. He is constantly injecting himself and his own selling style into their sales processes. This type of manager interaction usually makes the customer suspicious. At times, this interference can even kill the sale. Often, John's interference hurts the rapport that has been built between the salesperson and the customer.

There is another sad and ironic aspect of this promotion. Since the new manger was a sales superstar, the sales people on his team usually have poorer sales figures than the new manager, which causes the manager to wonder what is "wrong" with his team. When the team's performance lags behind John's expectations, it causes John to become frustrated with his team members. His frustration only leads to further dysfunction within his team.

To add to these declining numbers, once John becomes a manager, he is taken off the sales floor, which leads to an even lower sales volume for the entire store.

This kind of negative spiral usually results in the store's sales volume decreasing, and an entire sale's team of unmotivated and disgruntled employees. Nobody wants this kind of situation to develop for their dealership and for any of their sales superstars. Yet, this kind of situation is common in car dealerships across this country.

The next time you are thinking about promoting a sales superstar to the position of sales manager, ask yourself if it is the best reward that you can give your salesman. Maybe your top salesperson only wants to sell, sell, and sell. Maybe he doesn't want to manage other people. In this type of situation, you may find the best reward is simply paying the person extremely well for selling and offering public appreciation for a job well done.

People are motivated by different things. Good management identifies what is important and rewards accordingly.

How you pay people is crucial in motivating and retaining your employees.

> *"If you pick the right people and give them the opportunity to spread their wings and put compensation as a carrier behind it you almost don't have to manage them."* **Jack Welch**

How you pay people is one of the most important aspects of running any successful business. Your dealership or business will be more profitable if your employees are: happy, motivated, and loyal. Fair pay for your employees is crucial in managing your dealership effectively. However, most dealer principles and managers rarely put much thought into constructing their employee's pay plans.

Structuring an effective pay plan or commission structure that keeps your employees happy, motivated, and loyal seems like a difficult task to accomplish. Many managers try to solve this problem by making their pay plans extremely complicated. But, like so many other things in life, it is best to K.I.S.S.- Keep It Simple Stupid.

The most important objective to achieve when structuring a pay plan is to align the employee's goals with the goals of the dealership or the business. Period. If you can accomplish this one thing, you will have taken a giant step in improving your profitability and your employee retention. Remember, HOW you pay people is much more important than WHAT you pay them.

- Do you want your employees to feel like they are part of the company? Incentivize them accordingly.
- Do you want to retain star salesmen for a long period of time? Incentivize them accordingly.
- Are there certain products (extended warranties, aged units, etc...) that you want your sales staff to focus on? Incentivize them accordingly.

Ask yourself one very important question. What exactly am I paying each one of my employees to do? In other words, are you incentivizing the most important thing or are you incentivizing something else?

When creating a pay plan it is important to *put first things first*. What is most important? Determine which task or responsibility is most important to each function within your retail or wholesale automotive organization and incentivize the hell out of your employees to exceed your expectations with regard to this "most important thing."

For example, many dealerships employ inventory managers. Typically, this person's job responsibilities include: organizing the frontlot, managing other porters, maintaining the appearance of the saleable inventory, plus countless other responsibilities. However, all of their other responsibilities will come to a screeching halt as soon as a vehicle goes missing. When this happens, all inventory personnel and many other dealership employees focus all of their energy trying to locate the missing vehicle. A lost or stolen vehicle is an enormous financial loss for any dealership. Therefore, it is easy to say that the *most important* responsibility of any inventory manager is NOT TO LOSE ANY VEHICLES. If you want your inventory manager to focus on inventory security, incentivize him to do so. You could offer bonuses for every month that the dealership's inventory is always accounted for. You could offer stiff penalties for any loss of inventory. If an inventory manager receives more money for security and less pay for lack of security, it is safe to assume that security will always be forefront in the mind of that inventory manager.

We can also look to the sales position for another example of rewarding the wrong behavior. A salesman's most important task is to sell. Sell. Sell. Sell. Unfortunately, we as managers, often fill up our sales people's time with non-sales activities. We all know that without sales, our organization would not survive. So, why do we do this? I think it comes from watching sales people when they have free time. We as managers rarely have free time so why should sales people? Maybe we cannot tolerate free time, so we assign tasks that will occupy a salesman's free time.

Being a salesperson is a high pressure, difficult profession, and most of the time the sales process can be very draining. If salespeople need breaks in order to perform or sell at their highest level, then they should have breaks. We should not care about how much break time they have. We should only care about how many units they sell. When a manager is managing their employee's free time, they are managing the wrong issue.

If salesmen are more effective by taking more breaks, let them have them. You can always measure the results.

Pay your employees appropriately, and they will manage their own activities. Sometimes, sales people can lose sight of their schedules. Sometimes, they might need a nudge or two. But for the most part, if salespeople cannot master their own time and energy, they are probably not very good and should be looking for a job somewhere else.

Each employee in your dealership has different assignments. For salespeople, that job is to sell, for managers, that job is to manage.

We spend a lot of time in dealerships teaching people how to sell, while we spend virtually zero time teaching people how to manage others. It doesn't matter how well people can sell, if they cannot **teach** and **motivate** their team to sell. This is why we promote our best salespeople, because we want them to teach others and multiply their efforts through the employees they are managing. This however requires a specific temperament and skill set.

What are the skills needed to effectively manage others?

"So much of what we call management consists in making it difficult for people to work." **Peter Druker**

"I simply dislike the traits that have come to be associated with 'managing'. Controlling, stifling people, keeping them in the dark, wasting their time on trivia and reports. Breathing down their necks. You can't manage self confidence into people. You have to get out of their way and let it grow in them by allowing them to win, and then rewarding them when they do. The word manager has too often come to be synonymous with control-cold, uncaring, button-down, and passionless." **Jack Welch**

Each manager has a particular set of tasks and a specific group of people they are responsible for overseeing. Accounting managers supervise the accounting function. Sales managers supervise the sales function. However, there are certain tasks that are shared by all managers.

- Managers must plan and organize.
- Managers must communicate.
- Managers must develop themselves and their employees.
- Managers must motivate.
- Managers must lead.

Managers must plan and organize.

Effective managers set the goals that others seek to achieve. They define the vision for their team or department. This requires the careful analysis of several factors. These factors include but are not limited to: past performance, available resources, the competitive environment, macro economic factors, and opportunity costs.

Once managers decide which goals are important, they devise plans to achieve these goals, divide that plan into attainable action steps, and assign different employees to the necessary tasks.

Managers must communicate.

Effective managers must be able to properly communicate with their team members. Great planning and organization will not matter if it cannot be communicated to the team members. Effective communication is achieved through clear and precise language. It is also important that the manager's nonverbal communication is not giving any mixed signals. In other words, do the actions of the manager match their words, or do they tell their team to "work hard" and then leave the dealership early every day? They must inspire their team with their words and their actions.

Effective communicators can convey their thoughts and their desired values throughout the entire dealership culture. If management's goals and shared values are understood by everyone, it makes it easy for even the lowest-level employee to operate on a daily basis. They can make decisions that are consistent with the desires and wishes of the people at the top of the organization.

Managers must develop themselves and their employees.

Effective managers are good teachers, and good teachers train their employees properly. Training is essentially teaching. Teaching is a concept we are all familiar with, yet very few of us can do well. Teaching another person a new skill can be difficult and frustrating, but it can also be very rewarding.

Your ability to teach must be preceded by a willingness to teach. You must care enough about your team members to want them to do well. You must want them to succeed. The best managers are passionate about wanting their employees to achieve greatness. They also have the patience and the communication skills needed to help them achieve that greatness.

Teaching others is a unique skill that requires continuous work and dedication. Ask yourself these questions:

- How much time do you and your managers spend teaching?
- How much time do you spend teaching your employees basic sales skills?
- How much time do you spend teaching your employees about the products they sell?
- Do you have formal classroom training sessions?
- Do you teach your employees the importance and functions of the other departments within the dealership?

Teaching takes time and effort. There are no easy short cuts to having properly trained employees; however, if you want to develop your employee's potential, you must make training a high priority.

Managers must motivate.

Because motivation is an essential element of good management, an effective manager MUST be able to motivate others. Great managers are constantly trying to find ways to motivate their team members. Great managers are constantly searching for ways to inspire their employees.

> *"People are not lazy; they simply have impotent goals- that is, goals that do not inspire them."*
> **Anthony Robbins**

If you want to inspire and motivate your employees, they will first have to trust you. Trust is earned, not given. Earning trust takes a long time, losing it takes a minute. So how do you earn someone's trust? This is easy; you make your actions match your words. In other words, you must "walk the talk." Trust is earned every day. It is earned in everything you say and everything you do. Motivation is a social process not an analytical one. Internal characteristics such as character and integrity will have the greatest impact on your ability to earn your team's trust.

Employees will quickly see through empty promises and meaningless words that are not backed up by action. Because of this, the best way to truly motivate others is to lead by example. If a manager comes to work early, stays late, works hard, and helps the other members of his team without hesitation, human nature dictates that others on his team will imitate his behavior.

Managers must lead.

"Inventories can be managed, but people must be led."   **Ross Perot**

One of the most important aspects of management is the ability to be a good leader. This is especially true within service organizations. At their core, dealerships are service organizations. Because of this, your success or failure will be determined by how well you recognize and satisfy your customers' needs. Manufacturing organizations rely on the uniqueness and quality of their products. Service organizations rely on their ability to service their customers. Keep in mind that the services provided by your dealership are actually supplied by every single employee in the dealership. Therefore, your employees are the real "product" of your dealership. The better your employees are, the better your dealership will be. This requires leadership. If you want your employees to follow you, you must have a vision and then communicate that vision to your employees.

When we think about good leaders, several qualities quickly come to mind. Most leaders possess similar personality traits, including: honesty, integrity, and an internal drive to succeed. Leaders must also have a solid foundation of knowledge and skills if they are to lead effectively. Most are well trained in management techniques. They possess an ability to communicate effectively. They also possess an immense amount of knowledge about their particular industry and company.

The two most important aspects of being a good leader are the ability to create a vision for the organization and the ability to communicate that vision throughout the entire organization.

Create the vision.

> *"The very essence of leadership is that you have to have vision. You can't blow an uncertain trumpet."*
> **Theodore M Hesburgh**

As a leader, you must create the vision that you ask others to follow. If you supply your employees with a compelling vision, one that speaks to their dreams and aspirations as well as their wallets, you will have a highly motivated workforce. Creating a vision is similar to setting your company on the "correct path." However, finding the correct path can be a difficult task. There are tough decisions to be made, and you will need to use all of the resources at your disposal to make these decisions.

To create a vision for your company's future, you must start by analyzing your company's past performance. This requires digging through historical data and asking yourself several questions about the data. The answers to these questions will help paint the picture of your dealership's financial well being. These questions will show you which departments are performing well and which areas need assistance.

Some examples of the questions you should ask:

- How has your dealership or organization been performing during the past 6 months?
- How about the past 2 years? The past 5 years?
- What do the month-to-month sales trends look like?
- What do the year-to-year sales trends look like?
- What do the expense trends look like?
- Has revenue been trending upward or downward?
- At what rate is it changing?
- How does your dealership's profitability break down among the different departments?
- How have these departmental trends changed throughout the past few years?

Vision creation requires spending time thinking about factors outside of your dealership. This includes having a clear view of the economy and other macro trends affecting your dealership.

- What is the current trend in worldwide car sales?
- What is the trend in US car sales?
- How is the overall economy doing?
- How strong is consumer spending?
- What is the current unemployment rate in the United States?
- Are the credit markets functioning properly?
- Are there any new developments that are coming to the industry that will affect your dealership in particular?

Creating a vision for your dealership requires analyzing your competition.

- Where does your dealership stand compared to your competition?
- What are the things your competitors do well?
- What kind of things do they do poorly?
- What kind of things do they do differently?
- Why do they do these things differently?
- How is your competition viewed by your customer?

Then you need to take all of the historical information and synthesize it into your vision for the future.

- What will the future of your dealership look like?
- How will your dealership be positioned in the future?
- Does that vision properly correspond with what the future environment will look like?

These are some of the questions that you need to ask yourself to formulate your vision. In the brainstorming stage of any endeavor, new ideas will pop up quickly. These are going to be the seeds of your vision. **Write these ideas down.** Once you have formulated answers to these questions, your vision for your dealership or organization should be getting much clearer. Once your vision is complete, **you must write it down**. Writing your vision down will make your vision come to life. You don't want to forget anything important, and you also want your vision to be crystal clear so it can be effectively communicated. Writing it down will accomplish both of these goals.

The vision has to be communicated.

> *"Simplicity is absolutely essential to getting the environment, the vision, the plan, across to large groups of people at all levels, both inside and outside the company."* **Jack Welch**

Any vision that is developed but isn't effectively communicated to every member of the organization is virtually worthless. In order for a vision to have power, in order for a vision to have impact, it MUST be communicated and internalized by every member of the leader's organization. Visions can be simple or they can be complex, but they MUST be understood and internalized by others, if they are to be effective.

The best visions represent general themes or ideas, rather than a specific achievement or goal. They should be easily understood by your customers. Further, a vision should be able to communicate the values of your company to your customer in only a few words. Visions that are clear can even be communicated with very short slogans. Examples of this would include:

- Quality is Job 1- Ford
- Get More- T Mobile
- Your friend in the digital age- Cox Communications
- The most trusted name in news- CNN
- It's everywhere you want to be- Visa

These corporate slogans quickly explain the company's vision. These slogans tell the world which attributes are most important to these companies. Still, for these visions to be truly effective, they must be internalized by every employee in your organization.

There are several things leaders can do to ensure their visions are understood and internalized by employees. First, leaders must constantly promote their visions. Of course, this requires that the leader internalize the vision. Once leaders internalize their own visions, they can "walk the talk." In the retail automotive industry, this is one of the most effective and well regarded styles of leadership.

How should you promote your vision to the other employees? First, you must let them SEE your vision within you and with your actions. The qualities and the attributes that you want for your dealership must be demonstrated by you at all times. For example, let's say the vision you have for your dealership is focused on quality. You believe that if your dealership truly committed to a higher quality standard, then you would acquire more market share, have more satisfied customers, and have higher profits. However, when you are asked by your mechanics to spend slightly more money on reconditioning your used cars, you choose the lower quality path. When given the choice of improving your customer service department or saving a few extra dollars, you choose to save the dollars. When given any choice, you constantly choose the lesser quality route.

Your day-to-day actions have more impact on how well your employees are internalizing your vision than any other form of communication you may have with them. In other words, if you want your employees to work their butts off, then YOU need to work your butt off. You need to be the first one in the door and the last one to leave every day. This is what works. This is what motivates employees. Actions always speak louder than words. When your employees see that your actions match your words, then and only then, will they follow.

Things to keep in mind about managing and leading other people

- If a person can perform a task well, it does not necessarily mean they can also manage other people who are performing that same task.
- The ability to effectively manage other people requires a unique skill.
- Different people are motivated by different things.
- Praise often, praise in public, and praise in a timely fashion.
- How you pay people is extremely important.
- Always consider what you are paying your employees to do.
- Are you properly incentivizing the most important things?
- Before you promote someone to the position of manager, ask yourself, "Does the employee have the temperament and ability to be an effective manager?"
- Trust is earned every day.
- Managers must plan and organize.
- Managers must communicate.
- Managers must develop themselves and their employees.
- Managers must motivate.
- Managers must lead.
- Leadership requires creating and effectively communicating a vision.
- When brainstorming ideas, always right them down.
- The best form of leadership is leading by example.
- Leading by example requires your actions to match your words.

A tiny bit about the Used Car Business

Be nice to everyone, but especially the office personnel.

In college, my marketing professor loved to stress the importance of being professional and nice to everyone you meet during a sales call. Whether you encounter the Vice President of a company or the janitor, be nice and pleasant to everyone, because you never know when that person will make or break a deal for you. I took his lesson to heart because it sounded like good common sense. Twenty years later, I can easily say he was 100% correct. His words echo through my mind every time I encounter someone during a visit to a dealership.

During my career I have witnessed several instances in which someone's unprofessionalism cost them money and even damaged their reputation. One particular incident quickly springs to mind.

I was visiting a UCM at a family-owned dealership on a Monday morning. I was there to pick up a few trade-in vehicles that I had purchased from him over the weekend. As I was completing my paperwork, the UCM and I sat in his office chatting about the weekend and drinking coffee. We were also watching a reconditioning vendor who was making a complete fool of himself. The UCM explained to me that this vendor had visited him on Friday and tried to convince the UCM to use his services. The UCM told him to "come back on Monday and I will have some work for you, and we will see how well you perform." Now the vendor was back at the dealership. However, he didn't come directly to the UCM's office when he entered the dealership, instead he walked directly over to talk to the very pretty young lady who was wiping down the vehicles that were parked in the showroom.

The vendor was not merely saying "hi", he was actively and blatantly hitting on the young woman. His body language and demeanor displayed his intentions for the entire dealership to witness. I asked the UCM if he was going to put a stop to this and he simply replied "no way, I want to see this." Almost on cue, the dealership's owner and the father of the 16 year old girl walked directly over to the vendor, exchanged a few words, and then proceeded to escort the vendor out of the dealership's door, holding him by the collar of his shirt. I did hear the final words the owner yelled at the vendor as he threw him out of his dealership. He said, "Don't let me catch you around here again."

Although this was entertaining to watch, I'm sure it was not a very pleasant experience for the vendor. Not only was he humiliated, he also lost a potential customer that could have generated thousands of dollars in revenue for his company. Still, it is hard to feel bad for this reconditioning vendor, since it was his own unprofessionalism that led to his being escorted out of the dealership.

We can never know which person will make or break a deal for us, we can never be certain who might have influence over the decision maker, so be nice and act professional to everyone you meet. This is not rocket science, it is just common courtesy. Unfortunately, common courtesy is not very common these days. In other words, you will stand out from the pack; if you are simply courteous to the people you meet.

- Greet everyone with a smile.
- Try to learn people's names.
- Call people: Mr, Mrs, Miss, unless they tell you to use their first names.
- Say please and thank you.

"It's nice to be important, but it's more important to be nice." **Author unknown**

Although it is important to be nice to everyone, over the years, I have learned that it is especially important to be nice to the business or title office personnel at any dealership. I have always found title offices to be fascinating places. They are typically staffed by women and the tenure of an office employee is much longer than your average dealership employee. Most of these women work extremely hard and have to tolerate all types of craziness throughout the day. From dealing with angry customers to dealing with a state's department of motor vehicles, office personnel have a tough job.

Because office personnel have a difficult job, they often have short fuses when it comes to improper procedures or incorrect paperwork. Things like this can easily place you on a person's "bad side." This is never a good idea, especially with title personnel.

As a wholesaler, much of your livelihood depends upon your ability to expedite the payment processes of dealerships. Dealerships, like anyone else, want to hang onto their money as long as possible. Because the business office is usually the department that can get a wholesaler paid quickly, I made sure to treat every one of my dealership's business office contacts with complete respect. I would also bring them Christmas and birthday presents, but showing day-to-day pleasantness got me further than all of the presents combined. When other wholesalers were "waiting on a second signature from the manager who was gone for the day," I would be at my bank with a check in my hand. Simple kindness and respect worked every time.

As a used car manager, your business office can be your biggest ally or one of your biggest enemies. Constant care should be taken to assure that you are always improving your relationship with the business office. Conflicts will arise, as they always do, but handle them with a spirit of cooperation and respect, and your dealership will be a more effective and pleasant place to work.

Be nice to everyone, but especially office personnel.

Time Management

As used car professionals and UCMs, the way we manage ourselves and our time is as important as how we manage other people.

> *"If you want to make good use of your time, you've got to know what's most important and then give it all you've got."* **Lee Iacocca**

Let's face it, we are busy people. The retail car industry is not an industry people should join if they do not like being active, and can't handle pressure. Our industry moves very quickly. It seems priorities are always expanding until our day is completely filled.

Do you find yourself constantly behind on your "to do" list? Are you working longer hours? Are you working longer hours and still falling behind?

There are two different views about time management. There are those who recommend planning everything. They use: calendars, day timers, cell phone alarms, Blackberries, and countless other "techniques" to buy themselves more time in their day. Every minute of their day is planned. Unfortunately, this technique is difficult to adopt for people who work in the car business because we deal directly with the consumer. If you are in a customer driven, retail environment, you are often at the mercy of the consumer's time schedule, not your own.

The other time management strategy tries to eliminate daily tasks rather than simply trying to organize them better. This is the more effective approach for those of us in the car business.

The most valuable resource we have is our time.

Time is our most valuable resource. We only get 24 hours a day and some use their 24 hours more wisely than others. Our industry is very competitive; the people who manage their time most effectively will always win.

How do you eliminate tasks from your daily schedule? Most people feel that everything they do is necessary. Further, they believe that if they don't perform a task, it will not get completed.

In order to take control of your schedule, you need to make two lists. Yes, you need to write them out. Seeing things visually will help you gain control over your daily activities.

1- List the most important aspects of your job. Things that you have to accomplish on a daily, weekly, or monthly basis. These tasks are *mission critical* to your job. Rank each task with a 1, 2, or 3. The tasks ranked with a 1, are the most critical and 3 being the least important.

2- Create a list of your daily activities. You cannot get to where you want to go in life if you do not know where you currently are. Further, you will never gain control of your schedule unless you know how you are actually spending your time. This exercise will give you an immense amount of insight into your actual routine. Keep a record of your daily activities for one week. Yes, write it down. Do NOT rely on your memory for what you "think" you do on a daily basis.

Once you have your daily activity list, you will need to combine it with your ***mission critical*** list. Mark each task with the corresponding 1, 2, or 3 classification. In other words, if it is a task that relates to a 1 on your mission critical list, mark the activity with a 1. Continue until you have all of your daily activities coded. If an activity does not match any of your mission critical items, mark them with a 4.

There is one last step. Everything on your activity list marked with a 3 or 4 must be eliminated as soon as possible.

Some of your 3 and 4 activities can probably be eliminated; others will need to be delegated. Delegation may require you to spend some time training others, but this will be time well invested. Having more things to do does not make you more effective, or make you more money; it just makes you busier. We are very busy people with countless priorities trying to capture our precious time. Since our time is so valuable, we must focus on those things that are most important. Those things that are ***mission critical***.

Have you ever spent your day performing tasks that were truly unimportant and avoided doing tasks that were truly critical? We all have. We all have a tendency to procrastinate things we do not want to deal with, such as a "problem vehicle" or that "problem customer." We want to feel busy and feel like we are working hard. This causes us to spend our time doing things that are not mission critical.

"To do two things at once is to do neither. "
Publius Syrus

To solve this problem, you must first limit your daily tasks to only those things you have ranked with a 1 or a 2. Second, spend your time working on things that are mission critical. Think to yourself, "If I only accomplished 1 thing today, what would be the most important task to accomplish?" Third, put that item at the top of your To Do list and complete it to the best of your ability before continuing on to any other items on your To Do list.

Finally, give yourself realistic deadlines. Don't merely write that you need to get something done, put a time limit on your activity. If you do not limit the amount of time you spend on a task, you will waste valuable time. Have you ever had one of those days when you only had a few things to accomplish, yet it took you all day to finish what should have been a few trivial tasks? This is due to Parkinson's Law which states *"work expands so as to fill the time available for its completion."* If you have one task or ten tasks to perform in a given period of time, each task will take as much time as you allocate to it. So, give yourself deadlines and stick to them.

- Time is your most precious resource, manage it accordingly.
- Eliminate tasks that are not mission critical.
- Do the most important thing first.
- Focus on one task at a time.
- Give yourself deadlines.

In the Used Car Business, sometimes you have to change jobs.

Managing yourself doesn't mean just effectively managing your time, it also means being proactive when managing your career as a used car professional.

Employee turnover is an unfortunate aspect of modern day America. According to the Bureau of Labor Statistics, the average person between the ages of 21 and 42 will change jobs between 7 and 10 times.[i] Employee turnover is even more commonplace in the car industry. This is especially true for UCMs, where changing jobs is part of the normal course of business.

There are some UCMs who have held the same job for decades. To those of you who have experienced an enormous amount of job security, I say "congratulations." For the other UCMs who have had to deal with continuous job changes, I say, "be prepared for more."

> *"The more things change, the more they stay the same."*   **French Proverb**

Change is an inevitable part of life. Change is also a major contributor to stress. In fact, the definition of stress is "the body's reaction to change." This is true whether you initiate the change yourself or the change is thrust upon you. This is true whether the change is received as positive or negative. Obviously we would like more positive changes in our life, but even positive changes will cause stress. If change is inevitable, and all change causes stress, what can we do to alleviate the stress derived from the changes in our life? The answer is to be prepared.

No one wants to live in a constant state of "ready to lose my job," however the more we are prepared for change, the better we are at adapting to our ever-changing environment. If our environment is not going to adapt to us, we must adapt to it. There are several things that a UCM can do to be proactive about the possibility of job loss or change.

Keeping your resume up to date is the first step. Do not wait until you are looking for a new job to update your resume. As I mentioned earlier, we are busy people, with a lot of things on our minds. So it is often difficult to recall the specific information about past jobs and responsibilities necessary to enhance our resumes. As soon as something changes about your job responsibilities, document it while it is still fresh in your mind. For example, if you receive a promotion or take on a new responsibility at work, immediately document this experience on your resume.

Further, your resume should contain more than just your job titles and your basic responsibilities. As UCMs we have certain metrics that we are responsible for achieving. You should include these in your resume, because these statistics will help paint the picture of how well you perform the functions of being a UCM. For example, including past sales statistics will help demonstrate your ability to sell cars.

- Did you break a single month sales record? Document it.
- Did you help the dealership achieve a new level of CSI scores? Document it.

- Do you have an exceptionally high inventory turn at your dealership because of a process you implemented? Document it.
- Were you recognized by the dealership or your team for some accomplishment? Document it
- Did you receive a customer letter demonstrating your excellent customer service? Document it.
- Have your actions dramatically reduced your dealership's reconditioning costs? Document it.
- Have your dealership's profit margins increased because of your actions? Document it.

By including specific accomplishments on your resume you will separate yourself from the competition when it comes time to look for a new job.

In the Used Car Business, sometimes other people change jobs.

When people leave your dealership, it is vital to perform an exit interview. Employee turnover is a common occurrence in the car business. Employee turnover not only damages overall employee morale, it is also extremely expensive. We spend a lot of money recruiting new employees. Then, we spend even more money training those employees. With all of the money spent on employee recruitment and development, it is important for the dealership to understand why they are losing employees.

Exit interviews are an excellent source of information for the management of any dealership. Employees are more apt to provide honest information and insight once they have decided to leave your organization. Employees who have already received their last pay check have nothing to lose by being honest. Further, the dealership has everything to gain from their insight.

Exit interviews also provide feedback to help you determine how your management team is actually performing. If an employee has a serious issue with a manager, it will usually be uncovered during an exit interview. You might even find managers who are doing an excellent job and deserve praise and recognition.

Exit interviews also provide data to analyze trends. Although turnover is high in the car business, it can always creep higher. Dealerships must know how their turnover rates compare to their competition. If turnover at your dealership begins to outpace your competition, you may have a serious problem. Analysis of your exit interviews should provide you with clues about how to reverse this type of situation, or at least slow it down.

It is also important for employees who decide to leave the dealership to leave with good thoughts about you. Your former employees will go to work at other places and they will continue speaking with their family and friends. In other words, they will continue to influence the purchase decisions of several people. You want your former employees to be a force of positive advertising for your dealership, not negative advertising. Just because a job at your dealership didn't work out for the employee, doesn't mean they can't spread the word about the positives of your dealership. Try to remember "what goes around comes around". These words ring true in our industry.

I know one General Manager who sends a hand written letter to each of his former employees thanking them for their service. He lets them know how much he appreciates all of their efforts. This simple act has resulted in numerous car deals from referrals originating with employees who are no longer with the dealership. In other words, he is still getting results from people who no longer work for him.

A tiny bit about the Used Car Business

The $100,000 Corolla

For a financial fraud to occur in a dealership, or in any organization, it usually requires the combined efforts of at least two individuals. These individuals need to have access to a company's financial records. In a dealership environment, this means the General Manager, the Comptroller, and the Used Car Manager. Unfortunately, when all three of these people conspire to commit a fraudulent activity, it can be very difficult to uncover. That is precisely what happened to create a $100,000 Toyota Corolla.

The $100,000 Corolla started out like most frauds-small. The three managers merely wanted to make a little extra monthly bonus money. In order to do that, they needed to "hide" some expenses. There are several places to hide money in a car dealership. The easiest place to hide money is usually in the used car inventory. This is mainly due to the inexact nature of used car valuations. These three managers knew that, and working together, they added a few thousand dollars onto the cost of a Corolla. Not just any Corolla, the Corolla they chose was 10 years old and barely running. The car was a piece of junk. Once they were successful the first time, it became easier and easier for them to continue adding expenses to the Corolla when it came time for them to receive their performance based bonuses.

Uncovering fraudulent activities is difficult to do, but one of the best weapons against inventory based fraud is conducting an inventory audit. This dealership's owner did insist on a yearly inventory audit. However, because the top three managers in the dealership were instigating the fraud, they had first-hand knowledge of when the audit was to take place. The three men simply reallocated the Corolla's costs across the entire used car inventory a few days before the audit. After the audit was completed, they moved the costs back to the Corolla.

When the fraud was eventually uncovered, the Toyota Corolla's expenses were well above $100,000.

How are you handling inventory audits at your dealership?

For more information about preventing fraudulent activities within your dealership, please visit www.UsedCarVoice.com.

Preventing Fraudulent Activities

In the car business, we work long hours. We also work most days of the year. Rarely do you meet a used car professional who takes much time off. This trend has increased in the past few years as dealerships have downsized dramatically. One employee is often asked to perform the same functions that were once the responsibilities of 2 or even 3 employees. With so much work to be done, it is easy to see why dealerships do not actively ask their employees to take time off. However, this practice will eventually hurt the profitability of your dealership. Non-stop work usually leads to ineffective and burnt out employees. Non-stop work is also a common component in committing theft or other fraudulent acts.

Beware of the employee who NEVER takes any time off.

Fraud and **theft** are 5 letter words that will ruin the day of any dealer principle. Running a profitable dealership is a challenging task. Having a large fraud or theft problem can make this challenge nearly impossible. When margins are decreasing and sales are declining, a large theft or fraud problem can even cause a dealership to close its doors.

I know it is difficult and even uncomfortable to imagine that some employees are going to steal. It is an unfortunate and ugly aspect of not only the car business but every type of business in existence today. People steal for multiple reasons. Some even have altruistic reasons behind their theft, such as a sick relative they are trying to care for. However, whatever their reason for stealing, it is important to accept that theft is a common occurrence and proactive steps should be taken to prevent fraud from happening and detect it when it does happen.

Two of the most effective internal controls a dealership can implement to prevent and detect fraud is enforcing a mandatory employee rotation program and mandatory vacation time. These steps are essential, *especially with employees who have financial responsibilities.*

Employee Rotation

Employee rotation will help eliminate fraudulent activities and increase morale. It will also result in a more efficient and effective work force. Employees can quickly become bored with routine tasks. This behavior is most obvious in the title and business offices of dealerships. Many of you have business office employees who work on the same task every single day. They do only Accounts Payable or Accounts Receivable. We narrow our employee's skill focus because many skills, such as title completion, improve with practice. We want our title clerk to focus on titles, so she becomes an expert. We want our accounts receivable clerk to focus on receivables, so she becomes an expert. But what happens if that employee gets sick or leaves the dealership? What happens when that employee becomes bored at her job? What happens when that employee wants to steal?

Employee rotation allows your employees to learn and acquire new skills. Rotations keep minds fresh and excited and are a great cure for boredom. When employees rotate jobs they acquire a much deeper understanding of their own positions as well as other job functions. For example, imagine how much better your business office would run if everyone knew how to do everyone else's job. If one person was out sick, the office would still hum along like a fine tuned machine. That is efficiency.

Further, employee rotation is an easy but effective way to implement checks and balances throughout your dealership. The mere presence of employee rotations will be enough to discourage many people from attempting any fraudulent activities. In other words, if you know another trained employee is going to be looking through your records, you will be less likely to falsify them.

Mandatory Vacations

"A vacation should be just long enough that your boss misses you, and not long enough for him to discover how well he can get along without you."

Anonymous

Mandatory vacations work in the same manner as employee rotation. The logic is simple. For people to continue their fraudulent practices, they need to be present at work. They need to be actively involved in keeping the fraud going. This becomes nearly impossible when they are on vacation. Because of this very reason, many frauds are uncovered when employees are out on vacation.

One of my favorite examples of this kind of fraud detection involves a mid-volume domestic dealership that had a very successful secondary and subprime lending operation. Their subprime finance manager, whom I'll call "Greg," ran an exceptionally smooth department. Fortunately for Greg, his dealership had a wonderful connection to a lending institution that virtually guaranteed any customer would receive financing. The credit might be expensive for the customer, but they would not be denied credit. Greg's subprime financing skills helped the dealership sell a high volume of used cars. Management loved Greg even more because of his work ethic. He was always at work; he never took any time off.

Unfortunately for Greg, he had some minor health problems and had to spend a few days in the hospital and away from the dealership. One of the other managers, I'll call him "Bill," filled in for Greg while he was gone. Everything was going smoothly until Bill was approached by a frantic customer. The customer was so frantic because he had forgotten to give Greg the $100 that Greg needed to get the customer's financing approved.

Bill was confused by this customer's statement because the dealership's finance department approved everyone regardless of their credit (this was in much easier credit times). Bill also knew the dealership had no such $100 fee for getting customers approved. Bill assured the customer they would receive financing and the customer left the dealership confused but happy. Bill then started calling every customer Greg had recently dealt with. Bill was shocked to find out that every single customer had given Greg $100 to assure their financing. Hundreds of customers were charged a $100 "fee" by Greg. Greg was charging people $100 to provide them the same service they would have received if they gave him nothing.

Needless to say, Greg was immediately fired upon his return to work. His theft was uncovered because he was forced to take time off from work. Nothing fancy, just a little time away, was all it took to expose Greg's fraudulent activities.

Mandatory vacations also have another positive effect on your dealership. They help eliminate burn out in a business that can be challenging and difficult at times. It is important that your employees have a chance to recharge their batteries. No one can live on work alone; people need a break. Countless studies have shown that most employees return from vacation with more excitement for their job and better focus on their job.

Making employees rotate positions and take vacations will make your dealership more efficient and help prevent and uncover fraudulent activities. If you are not currently implementing these procedures in your dealership please consider starting them as soon as possible.

- Employee rotation helps eliminate fraudulent activities.
- Employee rotation leads to a more skilled workforce.
- Employee rotation leads to a more efficient dealership.
- Beware of the employee who never takes a day off.
- Mandatory vacations can deter and uncover existing fraudulent activities.

The people you meet in the Used Car Business

What's in a name? There are some interesting names and nicknames in the car business.

I have done business with a guy named Guy.

I have done business with a guy named Daniel Daniel.

I have done business with a capitalist named Commie.

I have done business with a fat man named Tiny and a skinny man named Fats.

I have done business with a guy named *Hog* who had a partner named *Machine Gun*. I really enjoyed doing business with *Hog* and *Machine Gun*. I mostly enjoyed them because they would constantly refer to each other in the 3rd person. If they were walking my lot, looking for cars to wholesale, their typical conversation would go something like this:

Hog: "Machine Gun, what do you think of this Ford Expedition?"

Machine Gun: "I don't know Hog. What do you think?"

Hog: "Machine Gun, Hog doesn't know. I don't think Hog likes the color."

Machine Gun: "If Hog doesn't like the color, then neither does Machine Gun."

Hog: "Machine gun, did you just say you don't like the color?"

Machine Gun: "That is what Machine Gun said."

Hog: "I bet Machine gun also feels that the miles are a little high. That is what Hog thinks, because Hog thinks the miles are a little high for Hog's tastes."

Machine Gun: "I was just going to say that Machine Gun thinks Hog probably doesn't like the miles."

Then Hog would turn to me and say something like:

Hog: "Steve, Hog and Machine Gun can't make you an offer on that Expedition. Hog and Machine Gun don't like the color or the miles. But, Hog and Machine Gun will keep looking until we find something that Hog and Machine Gun want to buy."

I didn't always make money when I dealt with *Hog* and *Machine Gun*, but I always had a few laughs and a real good time.

Section III
SALES MANAGEMENT

Customer Service

The car business is extremely competitive. It seems everyone is constantly fighting for more market share and better customer loyalty. In order to achieve these goals we continuously speak to our employees about the importance of customer service. If we work in a franchise dealership we are receiving regular reports from the manufacturer about our level of customer service. As an industry, we put so much effort and energy into improving how our customers feel about us because we know one very simple thing; ***Treat your customers right or someone else will.***

We have all heard a thousand times that one disappointed customer will tell 10 or 20 people about their bad shopping experience. We know this to be true, so we work hard to avoid sending a customer out of the dealership angry. The reverse is also true. The greatest advertising your dealership can have is a happy and satisfied customer. This is the positive aspect of customer service that we should focus our energies on. Human behavior dictates that we avoid unpleasant experiences and repeat behaviors we find rewarding. If you want to turn new customers into repeat customers, make sure their experience at your dealership is a rewarding one.

Customer service starts as soon as your customer is greeted.

One of the most important places in any dealership is the front lobby. Your front lobby is important because it can set the tone for the customer's entire experience. It is where many of your customers will be welcomed.

When customers enter your dealership how are they greeted?

- Are they greeted by a salesman as soon as they step out of their car?
- Are they greeted by a salesman when they enter the lobby?
- Are they met by a greeter?
- Are they welcomed by the receptionist?

There are countless ways a dealership can welcome a customer. What is most important is that the customers are actually greeted.

Every dealership has their own unique way of making their customers feel welcome. Many dealerships list the names of the day's scheduled appointments. Some have televisions in their lobby and offer coffee or other drinks to their customers. Even though these amenities are small, they can make a huge difference in the customer's mind. What things do you do in your dealership to make your customers feel welcome? Is there anything else you could be doing?

Customer Service is everyone's job.

At one time or another, customers will interact with every department within your dealership. As managers, we have no control over which employee a customer may interact with. Therefore, we should instill our customer service values in all of our employees, no matter their position. Every employee in the dealership is important in conveying good customer service. Every employee must value customer service as one of their top goals if the dealership is to thrive. This includes everyone, from the General Manager to the receptionist, especially the receptionist.

"My dog can bark like a congressman, fetch like an aide, beg like a press secretary and play dead like a receptionist when the phone rings."
Gerald B. H. Solomon

One of the most overlooked, yet important, parts of the front lobby is a dealership's receptionist. The receptionist position is vital in the success of your dealership because the receptionist is often the customer's first point of contact. Therefore it is critical to properly hire and train people for this position. It is also important to verify how well your receptionist performs.

Is your receptionist fielding so many calls that her telephone lights up like a Christmas tree? If so, she is not a receptionist, she has become an operator. Operators dispatch calls. Receptionists welcome customers. In the customer's mind, the difference is enormous. Check your dealership's call volume and make sure it can be appropriately handled. Are there different periods of the day that the call volume is overwhelming? If so, you can increase staffing levels during these periods. Nothing is more frustrating for a potential or existing customer than being placed on hold for long periods of time.

It is also important to verify your receptionist's tone and mannerisms on the telephone. Is her phone style pleasing or off-putting to customers? Can she properly diagnose which employee a customer will need to speak with? These are important things to verify. I know many dealers who secretly verify their receptionist's performance by having a third party call the dealership or doing it themselves by changing their voices and using a random phone line. I think this is an important exercise and encourage all dealerships to secretly shop their receptionist. There are few things as important as managing your customer's first point of contact.

For your salespeople, customer service starts the second the deal is closed. Most salespeople think their work is completed at this point, but this kind of thinking leads to a lack of repeat customers. Salespeople who stay in contact and properly service their customers after the sale will build a large pipeline of repeat customers. Performing customer service, however, takes time away from your sales team's most important job, selling. So, when the size of the dealership is large enough, many of these responsibilities can be transferred to a customer service department.

Customer Service Department- To have or not to have, that is the question.

Most dealerships treat customer service in one of two ways:

- The individual salesman is responsible for handling customer service issues.
- The dealership hires an employee or several employees specifically to handle the customer service responsibilities.

Whether or not a dealership has a separate department that solely deals with customer service usually depends on the dealership's size. I would argue that even if your dealership is extremely small it is still important to have a customer service department. It might include only one person, or even a part time employee.

What is disappointing is that employees who oversee customer service are typically among the lowest paid employees in the dealership and are usually treated as an afterthought. It's easy to see why dealerships don't place superstars in customer service positions and why these positions typically pay less than others. Many dealerships view the customer service department (if they even have one) as a non-income producing department. Because of this, customer service gets fewer resources when compared to other departments, like sales or service.

Typically customer service representatives have more interaction with your customer after the sale than anyone else in your dealership. Why is this the person that dealerships choose to under pay and under develop? This seems crazy to me.

When thinking about customer service, it is important to ask yourself, "Where are you spending your money?"

- Dealerships pay thousands of dollars for advertising to get customers in the door.
- Dealerships pay hundreds of thousands of dollars for inventory that sits upon expensive real estate.
- Dealerships pay enormous electric bills so they can show off their inventory.
- Dealerships pay sales consultants thousands of dollars and managers even more money so they can sell cars.

Dealerships spend an enormous amount of money and sometimes something great happens... the customer buys a vehicle. FANTASTIC!!

After all the money and effort that goes into getting customers to buy a vehicle from you, why would you trust their future happiness to anyone other than someone who is passionate about customer service? Why would you put your customers in the hands of someone who doesn't provide excellent customer service?

Customer service is not sales. Car salesmen are always trying to sell. That's why we hire them. That's what we want them to be focused on. Selling, selling, and selling. Keep your sales staff focused on closing their current customers and keeping their sales pipeline full of potential customers. Keep them focused on the task of selling, as if your business lives and dies by how well they do their job. Because, your business will *live or die* by how well they do their job. It is a very difficult job, so let them focus on it.

Who will service your past customers if your sales team is focused on their current customer and their sales pipeline? This is where a customer service representative or a customer service department should take over.

There are countless responsibilities that a customer service representative can have.

- Sending small gifts or a card on special occasions (holidays, birthdays, etc...).
- Handling follow-up phone calls.
- Making sure a customer's visit to the service department was a happy and successful one.

- Making customers feel *so special* they wouldn't think of buying a car anywhere else.
- Making customers feel *so special,* they tell everyone they know how great your dealership is.

A customer service department's job is to take care of your most valuable commodity, your customers. Some people say their employees are their greatest resource. I think both employees and customers are extremely valuable. The truth is, you can have the greatest team of employees in the world, but if you have no customers, who will ever know? Your dealership will live or die by your customers. **Take good care of them!**

When dealing with customers, doing the small things right can make a big difference. If your customer service department is functioning properly, they can truly focus their energies on the smaller things about customer service that often get overlooked. Simple common courtesies can have a dramatic impact on how your customers feel about you. Why? It is probably because so few people exhibit common courtesies these days. Think about the last time you visited any retail store and were treated exceptionally well. It's difficult to do, because an exceptional level of service isn't the norm anymore in the retail industry. Actually, the standard for customer service has declined in most industries throughout the past few decades.

Do you want to separate your dealership from your competition? Treat your customers in an uncommon and courteous way. This kind of behavior should be a major goal for any customer service department. To this day, my wife still tells the story about the Honda dealership where she bought her first car. This dealership sent her a batch of cookies on her one year anniversary of buying the car. It was a small thing, but it made an enormous impact. She has gone on to recommend that same Honda dealership to everyone who has ever asked her for a dealership recommendation. That is a lot of advertising return for the cost of a plate of cookies.

Doing the small things right is difficult to do if you don't have a customer service department dedicated to these tasks. If you have a dealership large enough to support a fulltime person or department that is dedicated solely to serving your customers and you don't have anyone in this position, you should seriously think about changing this. If you have an under achiever who is paid very little working in your customer service position, *change this immediately*. Customer service associates take care of your greatest resource, train them and pay them appropriately.

Another large thing that often gets treated as a small thing is the *cleanliness* of the dealership.

Cleanliness

"So great is the effect of cleanliness upon man that it extends even to his moral character."
Count Benjamin Thompson Rumford

When it comes to maintaining a clean retail environment, we should take a lesson from two business titans. In the business world, it is hard to find two bigger names than Walt Disney and Ray Kroc, the leaders behind Disney and McDonalds. Both men were the inspiration and the driving force behind two of the largest corporate empires in the world. Both men had unique visions that transformed their respective industries. Both men also worked tirelessly to maintain the highest levels of cleanliness possible in their retail establishments.

Would you be surprised to learn that these two men shared a common bond when they were younger?

As fate or luck would have it, Disney and Kroc were stationed together in World War I. Not only were they stationed together, they were part of the same ambulance corps. As we all know, cleanliness is critical in emergency medicine. One could assume that maintaining a clean environment on the battlefield was the highest priority for any ambulance crew. Two young men, in the early stages of their lives, found themselves working in an extremely hostile environment. Further, they found themselves in an environment where cleanliness made the difference between life and death. Imagine the impact that must have had on them.

Both men took these lessons with them throughout their lives. They both became passionate about cleanliness. Keeping their facilities spotless became a trademark of both McDonalds and Disney. Both men consistently spoke and wrote about the importance of maintaining a clean environment for the success of any retail business endeavor. Toward the end of Kroc's life, he would visit each store personally. His main job was to check on the cleanliness of the facility. Nothing was more important to Kroc than pleasing his customers, and he knew the first way to displease a customer was to have them see a dirty restaurant.

Obviously, car dealerships will be dirtier than theme parks or restaurants. Restaurants serve food, and we serve vehicles that contain oil and gasoline. However, there are certain areas of your dealership that should be treated with the same care as a Disney theme park or a McDonald's restaurant. These include:

- The bathrooms.
- The employee's and manager's offices.
- The employee's and manager's desks.
- A coffee or food station.
- The inside and outside of every vehicle.
- Anywhere a customer might be.

We often forget that dealerships are retail businesses. We are a specialty retailer, but a retailer nonetheless. Americans are retail people. Americans LOVE to shop. American shoppers know what they like in retail shopping and one of those things is cleanliness.

"Quality, Service, Cleanliness, and Value." **Ray Kroc**

Having a clean dealership is important. The old saying goes "You only get one chance to make a first impression." What if your customer's first impression is of a bathroom stall overflowing in the men's room? What if the car the customer decides to test drive has trash in it? The customer might still like the car and may even buy it. But something will stop them telling everyone they know what a pleasure it was to shop at your dealership. It might exist only in their subconscious, but it will be there.

I recall one evening early in my career when I was an assistant UCM. I was walking the front lot with a salesman. As we were walking, I stopped and picked up a few pieces of trash. He asked me if that was my job. I politely told him that "making our dealership look as good as possible is every employee's job. The customer doesn't care whose job it is, they just see a piece of trash." He must have taken my words to heart because a few months later I heard him repeating the same speech to another salesman while picking up trash himself.

Would you rather shop at a place that looks like this?

Or This?

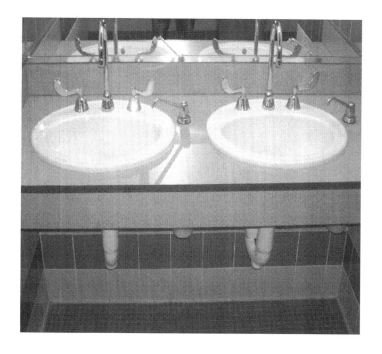

As managers we have countless opportunities to lead by example. Maintaining a pristinely clean environment can be implemented throughout the dealership by setting a solid example for your employees. It is also a value that can be easily communicated to employees. Simply tell them that having clean facilities is important to you, to the dealership, and should be important to the employee. As car professionals we spend a lot of time at work. Do you really want to spend that much time in a place that is dirty?

Ask yourself:

- Does my desk look like a hurricane tossed paperwork everywhere?
- How often am I in our dealership's bathroom and been disgusted by its level of cleanliness?
- How often have I found trash inside of cars that are saleable?

In the end, cleanliness is all about making the customer, as well as the employee happy. In today's competitive environment, providing excellent customer service and a clean working environment will separate you from your competition and make your dealership much more profitable in the long run.

Things to keep in mind about customer service

- Treat your customers right, or someone else will.
- The best advertisement for your dealership is happy, satisfied customers who share their feelings with their family and friends.
- Customer service is everyone's job.
- Greet and welcome every one of your customers.
- Customer service departments are an effective way to handle customer service issues.
- Doing the small things right can make a big difference.
- Make sure your dealership maintains the highest standards of cleanliness possible.

Questions to ask yourself about customer service

- Does everyone at my dealership know the importance of customer service?
- Are my customers being greeted in a manner that makes them feel welcome at the dealership?
- What things do I do to make my customers feel welcome?
- Is my receptionist overloaded with calls?
- Is my receptionist knowledgeable and pleasant on the phone?
- Do I already have a customer service department, or can one be implemented?
- Is my customer service department providing exceptional service?
- Are my customer service department personnel properly trained and well compensated?
- Is the appearance of my dealership inviting to customers?
- Does my dealership meet a customer's high cleanliness standards?

A tiny bit about the Used Car Business

Fletcher Jones Mercedes-Benz and excellent customer service

Fletcher Jones Mercedes-Benz in Newport Beach, California is the largest volume Mercedes dealership in the United States. This dealership's enormous success is partially due to their location. The demographics and the economic history of Newport Beach are very conducive to having a successful Mercedes dealership. However, what separates Fletcher Jones from other dealerships is their customer service. Fletcher Jones Mercedes Benz offers a level of customer service that is unrivaled in the retail automotive industry.

For example, some of the amenities that Fletcher Jones offers to their customers include:

- A FREE rental car when a customer's vehicle is in service for more than a day.
- A FREE ride to and from the local airport (John Wayne). Not only does Fletcher Jones take their customers to and from the airport, they wash and service their customer's vehicle while they are traveling.
- A FREE hand carwash, anytime, for as long as you own your car.
- FREE Starbucks coffee for their customers while they wait for service or a car wash.

I recently returned from a business trip and had the pleasure of sitting next to an executive from the Boeing Corporation. We chatted throughout the flight and had a pleasant conversation. Working for America's largest plane manufacturer meant this gentleman was constantly flying. His travel schedule was brutal, but he enjoyed his job.

I was working on this book while on the plane, so eventually our conversation turned to the subject matter within the book. I began explaining that I was writing a book about the used car industry. I had barely spoken, when he became excited to tell me something.

"You should write about Fletcher Jones." He almost screamed. "I bought my car there; I love their airport shuttle service. For someone like me (a frequent flyer), it is the greatest."

Little did he know, I was already planning to write something about the service provided by Fletcher Jones Mercedes-Benz. I have visited thousands of car dealerships in my lifetime and rarely am I impressed. Don't get me wrong, there are hundreds of outstanding dealerships across this country. These dealerships are exceptional in many ways, but I am talking about being **IMPRESSED**. I am talking about having your socks blown off. I heard from several people that Fletcher Jones was this type of dealer and represented the best level of service available in the dealership world. Very soon after moving to Orange County, I went to see for myself.

As soon as I pulled up to Fletcher Jones, I knew it was in a league all its own. The first thing I noticed was a line of 20-30 cars waiting to get into the dealership. This wasn't a Saturday afternoon in the middle of summer, during the easy credit years. It was early afternoon, on a Tuesday, during the middle of the economic tsunami that was the fall of 2008. How many dealerships across the country can say they had a line of customers waiting to enter their dealership during that period of time?

Many of the cars waiting to enter the lot were there for the free car wash service. Although some people look upon this as an unneeded expense, I see it as an excellent customer retention program and a unique value proposition. This level of service increases customer loyalty and referrals.

Their showroom was opulent and loaded with amenities. Of course, many highline dealerships have wonderful showrooms. What really struck me was the level of professionalism demonstrated by every employee I encountered during my visit. Each employee was truly passionate about selling cars and serving their customers. The entire dealership displayed a level of professionalism and enthusiasm that I have never encountered in the car business before.

This level of customer-focused service combined with top-of-the-line amenities creates an enormous amount of free, positive, word-of-mouth marketing. This brings me to the most powerful thing the Boeing executive said about the service at Fletcher Jones. He said, "I won't even look at another Mercedes dealership when I decide to buy my next Mercedes." He continued, "I tell everyone how great the dealership is." He was in fact, telling me at that moment, how great the dealership is. This is the power of exceptional customer service. This is the power of word-of-mouth referrals.

Fletcher Jones Mercedes-Benz offers a level of customer service that dealerships across the country should aspire to offer. Obviously, if you are a "buyhere/payhere" in a small town, the amenities you provide will be different from Fletcher Jones' amenities, but the enthusiasm and customer service focus can be the same. Remember, a superior level of customer service will separate you from your competition, whether you are selling Mercedes-Benz in Newport Beach, California or cars for under $2,000 in small town West Virginia.

Sales

"Nothing happens until a sale is made."
Tom Watson, Founder of IBM

A more traditional view of sales is one of a competition between the buyer and the salesperson. We often view the selling process as a struggle where someone wins and someone loses. Doesn't this view of the selling process lead us to believe that the customer must be FORCED to buy? It assumes that customers will not want to buy on their own. Why do we look at the selling process in this manner? Why do we view it as combative? Why do we see it as a process that needs to be manipulated?

Every manager and every dealership spends a considerable amount of energy and money on improving their sales numbers, sales processes, and their staff's ability to sell. Further, every individual sales person is also trying to sell more. They actively search for new techniques and more motivation. Our entire industry is made up of people who are constantly trying to find more information on how to improve their selling abilities. Unfortunately, most of the sales advice in the car business usually comes in only two forms. Managers and other experts tell you to:

Have the right attitude and **don't take NO for an answer.**

That's it. That is usually the extent of the advice we receive. We are told, "If you have the right attitude and never take NO for an answer you can be the greatest sales person in the world." We have heard this advice over and over again. We have attended hundreds of sales meetings where this philosophy is preached. Most of us, including myself, have preached it often. It seems so easy. If the secrets of success are so easy, why aren't more sales people successful? If it is this simple, why are so many sales people unhappy in their jobs?

Have the right attitude.

This is extremely common advice. You will hear it from almost every manager. You will find it in almost every inspirational and motivational book you read. They tell you to:

"Always have a positive attitude."

"Maintain a high level of enthusiasm."

"Spread your enthusiasm to your customer."

"Stay extremely optimistic."

"Visualize yourself making the sale."

"Never stop. Success is just one sales call away."

This implies that we are the only ones involved with the selling process. This advice completely ignores the wants and needs of our customers. This kind of advice teaches us that "if we trick ourselves into believing something, it will come true." This kind of advice teaches us that there is always a "mind trick" we can play on ourselves that will lead to success. We believe that if we can just focus on something positive we can make it through the rough parts of our week. We believe that if we can hype ourselves up enough, we can move mountains. However, this type of enthusiasm is short lived. It is the emotional equivalent of a caffeine high. It will motivate you for a short period of time, but it will eventually wear off.

To truly maintain your enthusiasm for selling, you must be motivated by things other than fancy slogans and mental tricks.

Why do you want to be successful at selling cars? Is it the money? If it were just the money, it would be difficult to maintain your enthusiasm and dedication over a long period of time. Your motivation for selling cars or any product must come from a place of honesty within yourself. Real, long lasting, motivation comes when you:

- Truly believe in the benefits of the product you are selling.
- Make your customer's needs and wants a priority.
- Have a burning internal desire to be an excellent sales person.

Truly believe in the benefits of the product you are selling.

Believing in the benefits of your product is critical to achieving a successful sales career. If you don't believe in the product you are selling, you will never live up to your true potential. If you don't believe in the product you are selling, it is probably time to look for other employment. For some in the car business, believing in their product is rooted in the make and models they receive from the factory. For example, a Ferrari or Lamborghini salesman feels an immense amount of pride in the quality of his or her products. This kind of enthusiasm is based on true feelings and is very powerful.

However, we can't all sell Lamborghinis. What if your "product" is a lot full of used cars? How can you believe in your product if they are all different and any one of them could break down at any moment? It is important to remember what **product** is actually being sold at your dealership. A customer can buy a car at any dealership. If they don't like your dealership, they can simply go down the street to your competition. The product your dealership is really selling is your ability to properly meet the customer's needs and wants. The product your dealership is really selling is the dealership's employees. What separates your dealership from every other dealership is how well the employees inside your store can form relationships with the customers who walk in your door.

You "believe" in your product when you believe in the people who work at your dealership and when you believe in the principles that guide your dealership. When I was wholesaling, it was difficult to be 100% certain about the mechanical condition of the cars that I sold-especially when I was dealing with high mileage vehicles. Some vehicles I would buy and sell over the telephone without ever seeing them. Yet, I was always 100% confident when selling these vehicles to other dealers. Why? Because I knew that I would make the customer completely satisfied with their purchases. If the car wasn't the way it was described or there was a problem with the vehicle, I would take it back. No questions asked. My customers would always be happy with the products they purchased from me. The car wasn't my product; my *service* was the product and my reputation for good service built trust. Having this type of confidence in your product will greatly improve your ability not only to build trust with your customer, but to be a better sales person as well.

Making your customer's needs and wants a priority. It's not about you, it's about them.

In every transaction, we are occupied with our own thoughts and actions. Individuals constantly think about their own situation and how it will affect the transaction. When we are selling, we think to ourselves:

- If he doesn't buy, will I be able to catch another customer before I go home for the day?
- I wonder what my commission on this deal will be.
- I hope I get my bonus this month.
- I think I presented the vehicle well.
- Should I mention another car as an option?

We spend much of our lives thinking about ourselves. When you are selling, you need to **stop** thinking about yourself. You need to shift your focus from your thoughts to your customer's thoughts.

Quite simply, you want to walk a mile in your customers' shoes, so you can see the situation from their point of view. Each customer has a unique set of needs and wants. This means that each customer has a particular reason why they will purchase something. The better you are at seeing the situation from your customer's perspective, the more in tune you will be with your customer's decision making process. Ask yourself:

- What is my customer's perspective?
- What does my customer want?
- How do I find out what my customer's perspective is?
- How do I find out what my customer wants?

First, you need to listen. Listening, however, does not mean simply being quiet while you patiently wait for your turn to talk. Listening does not mean thinking about a clever response while the other person is talking. What you really need to do is become an *active listener*. Active listening means asking your customer relevant and probing questions, then listening very carefully and intensely to their response.

Being an active listener means "listening" with all of your senses- not just hearing. Use your eyes. What is the other person's body language telling you? Are their arms crossed and closed or are they relaxed? What are you telling the other person with your body language?

One of the most important aspects of effective selling is the ability to build trust. Active listening is a guaranteed way to build trust with your customer. It lets the customer know that you really do care about serving their needs.

When dealing with customers it is important to only talk about things that are relevant to **them**. When you are speaking to a customer, you should constantly be asking yourself if what you are saying is relevant to the customer's needs and wants. We all have things we think are important when selling a vehicle, but, if it is not relevant and important to your customer, who cares? Remember, it is not about you, it is about them. Being an active listener allows your customer to tell you what is truly important to **them**. Once you know that information, you can simply point out solutions that will satisfy their true needs and wants.

If salespeople focus on satisfying their customers' wants and needs and truly believe in their products, they will have no problem closing deals. Believing with every fiber of your being that your dealership offers the absolute best used cars at the best price and offers every customer the absolute best service, it would be unimaginable to you for any customer to want to buy a vehicle anywhere else. This enthusiasm for your dealership and your products will be obvious to any consumer. Further, this kind of passion is extremely contagious and can easily be passed on to other employees as well as the salesperson's customers.

Don't take NO for an answer.

This is very *common* advice in the car business. It is also very *bad* advice.

Not taking **no** for an answer is the equivalent of bullying your customer into buying. This approach works best when the price of the object you are selling is very small. When the price tag is low, it doesn't matter how much skill the sales person has. It doesn't matter how rude the sales person is. If they "don't take **no** for an answer," they will probably have a lot of success selling. In other words, I can brow beat you into saying **yes**, if I am only selling you something that costs $1. If a sales person is persistent enough, and the product only costs $1, most people will buy whatever he is selling.

This approach does not work well in selling expensive merchandise. An automobile is usually a consumer's second largest purchase, after a home. When selling automobiles, we are usually dealing with high dollar amounts. This is not a type of transaction that lends itself to a bullying tactic. It may have worked 20 years ago when there was significantly less competition, but it does not work in today's environment. If customers feel bullied, they will go down the street to your competitor. Even if they do buy, but they felt bullied into their decision, they will not send any referral business to you. Bullying may work if you are selling something inexpensive to a customer you will never see again, but it is completely ineffective in selling expensive items and in generating referral clients.

Sometimes **no** really does mean **no** and a good salesman knows when it is appropriate to push and when it is time to move on to building relationships with other customers.

In writing this book I surveyed several high achieving automotive sales people. These are top performing sales professionals at their dealerships; real sales superstars. The survey included several questions, but my main objective was to determine which attributes these superstars felt were most important in achieving a high level of success in selling used cars (for a full list of survey questions, see Appendix 1). Two items were mentioned in nearly every survey as key ingredients for a successful career selling used cars. They were:

- The ability to build trust.
- The ability to obtain referrals and repeat business.

Building Trust

All of the sales superstars believed that the ability to build trust with their customers was key in their success as used car sales professionals. Building trust is achieved through putting the needs and the wants of your customers ahead of your own. Building trust comes from actively listening to your customers. Building trust comes from not bullying your customers. These are the steps needed to truly build trust with your customers.

It's all about referrals and repeat business.

All of the sales professionals told me that getting a high number of referrals has been vital to their success in the used car business. Referrals enable most of them to work strictly by appointments. Referrals help these professionals instantly build trust with a new customer. We are more likely to trust someone who comes recommended from a friend, than a salesman who randomly meets us in the parking lot. But how does a person go about increasing these referrals?

Referrals come from what happens after the sale.

One of the keys to making a lot of money in the car business, both retail and wholesale, is building a large referral base and repeat business network. This can only be accomplished by properly servicing your customer **after** the sale. In other words, once the customer has driven the vehicle off of the lot, there is still plenty of work to be done, but this work will be extremely profitable in the long run.

Maintaining contact with customers and properly servicing their needs after any sale is the best way to get referral customers. This is because so few people are ever contacted after they buy any product. Think about it. When was the last time you were contacted by a salesperson after you bought something? It is rare for salesmen to contact their customers after the sale. Maybe they are afraid they will hear bad news or buyer's remorse. We all work under the belief that "no news is good news." But this kind of thinking causes us to miss opportunities that build trust with our customers and maintain long standing relationships.

I recently bought a house that had been occupied by the same owners for over 20 years. I hired a cleaning service to perform a deep cleaning on the house before my wife and I were scheduled to move in. House cleaning is a physically demanding job, and this house needed a lot of work. It took a team of 4 people nearly 4 hours of constant work to get the house clean. Unfortunately, I had a meeting to attend and didn't see the crew when they left my house. However, to my delight, when I returned to my house it was so clean that it nearly sparkled. It looked amazing. I couldn't have been more pleased with their work. I was thrilled.

A few days later, I received a phone call from the owner of the company asking me if I was happy with the service that I received. "Absolutely," I said. I was pleased with the cleaning and even more pleased that she called me to make sure I was 100% satisfied. Knowing that each individual is different, and people can be very picky about the cleanliness of their homes, I assumed some people would be unhappy when she called them. I asked her "Do you get many complaints when you call your customers?"

She replied, "Not many, but I do get some. Usually they mention a part of the house that was not cleaned to their standards."

I followed up with, "Doesn't this create more work for you?" Then she said something very profound. "It actually creates less work for me." She continued, "I have found that customers are either happy or unhappy whether I call or not. If they are unhappy, I can immediately fix the situation, which makes people so happy, I get a ton of business sent to me. I used to have to advertise and spend a lot of time and money to get customers. Now they call me."

This really reinforced for me the power of simple follow up skills in getting referrals. She was exactly right. She was building her business in a smart way. She was building her business through referrals. In fact, I was a referral. I called her company because one of our friends told me that her company was excellent. I came to her already prepared to buy and to be satisfied with her product. Wouldn't it be great if customers walked into car dealerships with this same mindset?

Fear of receiving bad news is absolutely no excuse for not following up with your customers after the sale. Remember, customers are happy or unhappy whether you call or not. If they are unhappy, a call will give you a chance to fix the problem. You will have an opportunity to turn an unhappy customer into a happy customer. You have a chance to turn a customer who was going to tell 10 people NOT to buy from you into a customer who will tell 10 people to buy from you.

Some things to keep in mind about following up after the sale are:

- Wait a brief period before following up.
- Ask for referrals.
- If you can, spiff them.
- A one year anniversary is a perfect time for following up.

Wait a brief period of time before following up.

You should wait a short period of time after the sale before you contact your customer, but not too long. For example, you don't want to call the next day. The sale is too fresh in the consumer's mind, so you don't get enough "bang for your buck" for a follow up call that is too soon after the initial purchase. However, you don't want to wait too long either. If there is a problem, you want to catch it and fix it before the consumer becomes unhappy and starts telling other people about their unhappiness. I have found that about one week after the sale is a great time to contact customers. It gives them enough time to get a feel for the vehicle, yet it is soon enough after the sale to demonstrate that you care about their business long-term.

Ask for referrals.

Do you want more customers? Do you want to sell more cars? Do you want more referrals? Then you need to ask your customers for referrals. Your chances of getting something are greatly increased when you actually ask for it. In selling cars, I have found that an excellent time to ask your customer for referrals is just before they leave the lot in their newly purchased vehicle. After the finance paperwork has been signed, and the deal is closed, you should say something like "I hope you enjoyed my service today, if you did, please tell your friends and family about me. Thanks." That's it, nothing complicated, just old fashioned asking for the sale. I ALWAYS ask for the referral at the end.

If you can, spiff them.

One of the best ways to get people to do something is to pay them to do it. If you want your customers to send you referrals, pay them to do it. If your dealership allows for spiffs to be paid to your customers for referrals, you should advertise this every chance you get. Further, the spiff must be large enough to get the customer's attention. If your spiff is large enough, the next time your customer is asked by another person where they should go to buy a car, your customer will recommend your dealership.

A one year anniversary is a perfect time for following up.

It has been my experience, that one year from the purchase date is an excellent time to follow up with your customer again. It marks an important anniversary for them, and it is far enough in the future that it demonstrates a real desire by the salesman to properly serve the customer. This follow up can be a phone call or a card. I have found both to be highly effective in building customer loyalty.

Things to keep in mind about sales

- Having the right attitude and "not taking NO for an answer" will not produce long lasting results.
- Long-lasting results are achieved by truly believing in the benefits of the product you are selling.
- Long-lasting results are achieved by making your customer's needs and wants a priority.
- The "product" of your dealership is not only the vehicles, it is also the employees inside of the dealership and the dealership's set of values.
- If you don't believe in the "product" you are selling, you will never reach your full potential as sales professionals.
- If you want to succeed, build trust with your customers.
- It's all about referrals.
- Referrals come from what happens after the sale.
- Wait a brief period before following up.
- Ask for referrals.
- If you can, spiff them.
- A one year anniversary is a perfect time for following up.

A tiny bit about the Used Car Business

Dress Appropriately

"Clothes make the man. Naked people have little or no influence on society."   **Mark Twain**

Since the car business began, the suit has been the uniform of choice. Throughout the 20th Century, suits were the standard attire in dealerships everywhere. Quite simply, all car salesmen wore suits. Wearing a suit is an easy way to demonstrate to others your professional status. Still today, most sales and management personnel in automotive dealerships wear suits.

However, this trend is changing. The golf shirt is quickly becoming the uniform of choice. This casual trend is simply following the national trend. In the 50's it was impossible to find a white collar professional who wasn't wearing a suit. Then, "business casual" came along and people began to dress less formally. The creation of casual Friday has pushed this trend even further away from formal attire. With Americans dressing more casually, car dealership employees have begun to dress more casually.

Every dealership has its own dress standard. Some require suits, some require matching golf shirts, and some have no dress code at all. Whichever style your dealership chooses, always dress appropriately.

Avoid Inappropriate Jewelry

In addition to your clothing, you should pay attention to the amount of jewelry you wear. I know many people who love to wear a lot of jewelry, and in their private lives, people should feel free to wear as much jewelry as Mr. T, if they desire. What I am talking about is how much jewelry should be worn while working at a car dealership. Wearing excessive jewelry plays directly into the used car stereotype that most customers have in their minds. When customers see lots of jewelry on a used car salesman, they automatically think they are dealing with someone who will be fast talking and shady. Is it a fair stereotype? Absolutely not. However, we must always be aware of this stereotype. We must always be aware that if the customer sees us in this way, we will be at a disadvantage when it comes time to earn that customer's trust. With regard to jewelry, always err on the side of being conservative. Our goals are to:

- Sell more cars.
- Make more money.
- Enjoy our jobs.

Resembling a stereotype does not help us achieve any of these things. Resembling this stereotype only makes our jobs harder.

Make no mistake, what we wear communicates a great deal about us. Too much jewelry might say to the customer "I make lots of money." This could be acceptable, unless the customer believes that all of that money is coming out of his pocket. Is that the message you want to send to your customers? What might be a better message to send to your customer?

Let me make my point by telling a story about one of my favorite salespeople. I was working as a buyer for CarMax in Atlanta, where we employed several salespeople. There was one sales person in particular who I enjoyed speaking with whenever I had the opportunity. His name was Mr. Cho. Mr. Cho was retired and sold cars part-time at CarMax simply to get out of the house. Or as he put it "I get up, I walk the dog, I get bored, and so I come to work."

Mr. Cho was one of our top salesmen, even though he was only part-time. He certainly did not need the money. Although Mr. Cho was very humble and reserved, it didn't take long to figure out that he was also very wealthy. Mr. Cho owned one of the first McDonalds in Atlanta, and he also owned several liquor stores. He earned his money the old-fashioned way; he worked extremely hard for it. His son told me that his father frequently worked 18 hour days, seven days a week. He was a very hard worker, and his hard work paid off. He carried an American Express Black Card in his wallet and wore an extremely expensive Rolex on his wrist.

One day as I was walking through the showroom, I watched Mr. Cho greet a customer from the Ups list. He did something very odd, just before he shook the customer's hand. He took off his Rolex and stuffed it in his pocket. The next time I caught up with Mr. Cho I asked him about the incident. He told me that he takes his watch off every time he helps a customer. "Why"?" I asked. His response was unforgettable. He said "My customer is about to spend a lot of money. It's a decision that is very important to them. If they know my watch costs more than the car they are about to buy, I have given up the ability to empathize about price. They will no longer take my advice. It is not about me, it is about them. Always see yourself through your customer's eyes."

Mr. Cho knew about customers. He had made his livelihood by serving his customers. The immense amount of business knowledge he communicated to me that day was priceless. He was exactly right. When dealing with customers, it should **always** be about them and never about me. Mr. Cho never lost sight of this, even when he was working part-time during his retired years. He also knew how his jewelry and his style of dress affected his customer's mindset.

The bottom line is this, be mindful of your attire and the amount of jewelry you wear, especially if you are in sales.

"What a strange power there is in clothing."
Isaac Bashevis Singer

For those of you working in a business casual or casual environment, there are also certain rules that need to be followed. This can be illustrated by an incident that happened at a mid-volume independent dealership in Georgia that I used to visit when I was wholesaling. The dealership was in the process of hiring a new salesperson. Eventually, they found a candidate that they really liked. During the final interview, the management of the dealership instructed him that the dealership was business casual, but leaned more to the casual side. I have visited this dealership hundreds of times. Some employees wear khakis and a golf shirt, other wear jeans and a golf shirt, but everyone is always dressed appropriately. The new salesman must have noticed everyone's style of dress, as he was going through the interview process. However, when he showed up for his first day of work, he didn't mimic what the other employees normally wear. This new salesman showed up on his first day of work wearing jeans that had more holes than a slice of Swiss cheese and a half-shirt (a shirt specifically designed to only cover half of a person's stomach). He looked like he was going to a Motley Crue concert in the 1980's. Needless to say, the employee was immediately sent home and later fired.

When working in a business casual or casual dealership, remember:

- Casual does not mean unprofessional.
- Casual does not mean sloppy.
- Casual does not mean inappropriate.
- Casual does not mean unclean.
- Casual does not mean unshaven.
- Casual does not mean wearing unpolished shoes with holes in them.

Dealerships have a casual dress code so they can make their customers feel more comfortable. This is the test for all dealerships. Does your style of dress mirror your customers? In other words, if you are working in a buy here/pay here dealership in the middle of a small country town you should dress more casually. If you are selling new BMWs in Beverly Hills, California your dress should be more formal.

Your dress should mirror your customer, or as Mr. Cho put it, "It is not about me, it is about them."

Negotiation

> *"In business, you don't get what you deserve, you get what you negotiate."*　　　**Chester L. Karrass**

Much of your success as a Used Car Professional is directly related to your ability to negotiate. Negotiation is a major part of the used car business. As UCMs we are constantly negotiating. We negotiate with: customers, wholesalers, auctioneers, transport companies, mechanics, reconditioning vendors, other managers within the dealership, different departments within the dealership, and numerous others.

All human beings negotiate. Each culture negotiates differently, but whatever form it takes, negotiation is a common aspect of life. Some of our negotiations are simple. For example, we negotiate with our children to get them to eat their vegetables or to put on their pajamas, but most of our negotiations are more complicated. Fortunately, your negotiation ability can be improved through some personal analysis and a little work.

Determining your personal style of negotiation is the first step in improving your negotiation skills.

Negotiation begins with you.

You can't always choose who you will encounter during a negotiation. You can't control the other person's thoughts or actions. The only thoughts and actions you can control are your own. You can control how well you know yourself, and how well you prepare. Therefore, good negotiation skills must start with an examination of you. By learning more about your own preferences and negotiation style you will become a more effective negotiator. Your personal style will also guide your style of bargaining.

You can determine your personal style by asking yourself a few questions.

- What kind of person am I?
- Do I enjoy rigorous debate?
- Do I thrive on stress and conflict?
- Do I avoid conflict at all costs?
- Am I concerned about maintaining relationships with other people?

In other words, are you more **competitive** or **cooperative**? Most people fall somewhere between these two extremes but are closer to one than the other. Try to answer these questions honestly. There is no "right answer." A person who works in a cooperative way can have as much success, if not more, than a person who negotiates in a combative way.

We have all seen how negotiators are portrayed in the movies and on TV. They are usually yelling, pounding the table, and stomping out of a board room in an effort to win a negotiation. These characters are portrayed as ruthless and power hungry. They would certainly fall in the **competitive** category. Because of this stereotype, many of us feel that a competitive style would be the most effective way to negotiate. But, is this actually how a professional negotiator behaves?

In his landmark book about negotiating, Bargaining for Advantage, G. Richard Shell refutes this negotiation stereotype. He states that "two studies of negotiator behavior have revealed a more complex and accurate profile of how the average professional conducts himself or herself at the bargaining table. The first study covered American lawyers; the second looked at English labor negotiators and contract managers."

Shell's analysis of these two studies found that, contrary to popular stereotypes, within these two groups of people, the negotiators who were seen as cooperative were also viewed as being more effective than their peers who exhibited a competitive negotiation style.

Shell concludes that "The most effective of them (negotiators) displayed distinctly cooperative traits. The conclusion from both studies? Contrary to popular belief, perfectly reasonable, cooperative people appear to have a strong potential to become extremely effective negotiators."[ii]

The bottom line is this, if your personal disposition is cooperative by nature; use a cooperative style of negotiation. If your personal disposition is competitive by nature, use a competitive style. If you are still unsure about which style you are, simply ask those people who know you best if they would describe you as a more competitive or cooperative person. Chances are good, they will steer you in the right direction. Once you have discovered which type of "style" you bring to the bargaining table, you can begin to prepare for your negotiation.

Preparation is the key to a successful negotiation.

Out of all the elements of a successful negotiation, preparation is perhaps the most important. Thorough preparation is essential if you hope to achieve a successful outcome to any negotiation. Being prepared means playing different "what if" scenarios in your head. Excellent negotiators imagine and plan for every different kind of situation. They are always expecting surprises; so they are seldom surprised.

Being prepared means asking yourself an extensive number of questions.

- What is my goal in this negotiation?
- What is my opponent's goal?
- What is my position in this negotiation (are you in a position of power)?
- What is my opponent's position?
- What outcome would be considered a success for me?
- What outcome would be considered a success for my opponent?
- What outcome would be considered a failure for me?
- What outcome would be considered a failure for my opponent?

These and many other questions need to be considered and answered honestly to properly prepare for any negotiation. Answering these questions will help you define your goals for the negotiation. Examining and defining your ultimate goal in any negotiation is a very useful exercise.

"I believe in always having goals, and always setting them high."   **Sam Walton**

When setting your goals for any negotiation you must think carefully about those things you truly want. Make certain that you set your goals high, but keep them realistic. Be very specific with your goals and **write them down**. The negotiation process can be stressful and confusing. In those situations, it pays to have your goals clearly written down, so you can refocus your mind with just a glance at a piece of paper.

There are two major numbers we consider during a negotiation; the *goal* and the *worst case scenario*. You want to stay focused on the goal number. Why? The mind is a very powerful tool. The number you focus on will be the number that your mind will work toward. You want your mind working toward your goal, not toward your worst case scenario number.

The other important area to explore during your preparation is defining your relationship with your negotiation counterparty. Is this a one-time negotiation or is it a negotiation partner whom you will encounter again? If you are a wholesaler, you might negotiate with the same two or three UCMs for your entire career. Obviously, this kind of repeat customer should be handled differently than a person you will never see again.

"My father said: 'You must never try to make all the money that's in a deal. Let the other fellow make some money too, because if you have a reputation for always making all the money, you won't have many deals'."   **J Paul Getty**

Understanding what your counterparty wants during your negotiation is crucial. According to Shell, "effective negotiators exhibit a very important trait; the ability to see the world from the other party's point of view. Understanding what the other party wants is critical." This means you should spend a good portion of your preparation planning the negotiation from your counterparty's point-of-view. [iii]

What do they hope to achieve during this negotiation?

- What does a win look like for them? How about a loss?
- What does their worst case scenario look like?
- What are their strengths? What are their weaknesses?

Now that you have completed your preparation work, the actual negotiation can begin.

The person who speaks first, loses.

When it comes to negotiating a market transaction, such as the price of a car, the standard saying has always been "the one who speaks first loses." This implies that the person who offers the first price in the negotiation will lose. This would imply that we should never "open" a negotiation. Although this can sometimes be true, this belief disregards the powerful force that is anchoring.

Should you "open" a negotiation? The power of anchoring.

Anchoring is one of the most important aspects in any negotiation. The term refers to how human beings react to the first number that is introduced into a negotiation. Researchers have found that people move their expectations in the direction of opening numbers, whether that number is higher or lower than they originally expected. For example, if a customer wants to pay between $8,000 and $10,000 for a vehicle and the UCM offers a price of $12,000 as a starting number, the customer will automatically adjust her thinking toward the $10,000 number. This is the power of anchoring a negotiation.

There are environmental forces and industry standards that will also affect the anchoring process. It is important that we keep our negotiation parameters within these ranges. To illustrate, assume you are negotiating with a customer about the price of a vehicle. Let's assume the customer expects to pay an amount between $7,000 and $10,000. They have come to this conclusion by getting pricing information from Kelly Blue Book and NADA Guides. They have also been extensively shopping at other dealerships and have seen very similar vehicles within that price range. In this case, industry information and market forces have established an accepted range for the price of this vehicle.

If the UCM were to "open" the negotiation at $25,000, the customer would immediately walk out of the showroom. Why? Because the negotiation is outside of an acceptable range that has been established by the customer's research and the market dynamics for that vehicle. Any price outside of that range usually ends the negotiation. It is the UCM's responsibility to be ever aware of market fluctuations and conditions to avoid situations like these from occurring.

Should you "open" a negotiation?

The answer is... sometimes.

If you believe that your information about the established market is better than your customer, yes, you should open the negotiation. This will give you the advantage of anchoring the negotiation in your favor.

Once someone has opened the negotiation, you move into the information exchanging phase. In this stage, it is important to build rapport with your counter party. This is the part of the negotiation where communication skills are critical. Questions will be asked and answered by both sides, including:

- What does my counter party want out of this negotiation?
- What are my opponent's goals?
- What is my opponent's position?
- What outcome would be considered a success for my opponent?
- What outcome would be considered a failure for my opponent?
- Is my party authorized to sign and close the deal?

During the information exchanging phase, your listening skills are essential. Remember, active listening means truly focusing on the words and body language of the other person, not merely pausing while you wait for another opportunity to speak. If you listen closely to your counterparty during this information exchanging phase you will be able to answer the important questions that you have been contemplating.

Once you have exchanged information and know where both parties stand in terms of the negotiation, it is time for each party to make concessions and get commitments.

When making concessions, it is important to revisit your relationship with your counterparty. If you are negotiating with someone with whom you are planning a long term relationship, you need to make more concessions. You will want to address as many of their concerns as possible. During these kinds of negotiations, maintaining the working relationship should be the highest priority.

When the relationship with your counterparty isn't seen as a longterm relationship, you will be more inclined to concede fewer points to that person. In other words, if you will never interact with a person again after a negotiation, you are more likely to "go for the jugular." However, these types of scenarios are very rare. Most people you negotiate with will reappear in the future. This includes single retail customers who are only buying one car from you. They might have had a bad opinion of your negotiating style and tell all of their family and friends about their poor experience. For this reason, it is best to leave the other person believing they received a fair deal. To put it another way, leave some meat on the bone for the other person.

Once you have made concessions, the negotiation generally moves into the closing and commitment stage.

Some closings are easy and some are excruciatingly painful. Typically the closing is a reflection of the overall negotiation process. If the process has moved along smoothly and rapport has been built and each party has been truly listening to the other's concerns, then the closing goes very smoothly.

When it comes to closing, there are several techniques that are highly effective. Some of the most common closes are: scarcity, deadlining, good deal versus bad deal, and splitting the difference.

Scarcity

Scarcity is a way to influence a person's decision by implying that the supply is running out. An example would be, "We only have one Honda Accord at this price, and it will not last very long."

Deadlining

Deadlining works the same way as scarcity, but instead of supply you are dealing with time constraints. An example would be "The deadline for cash for clunkers is Tuesday. If you don't purchase before then, you will not receive a rebate for you vehicle."

Good Deal versus Bad Deal

This is just an extension on deadlining. This is when you offer a customer a fantastic deal. However, it is only available for a short period of time. Once that time period is over, the offer will be rescinded and a lesser deal will take its place on the bargaining table.

Split the Difference

This one is self-explanatory. You say "$11,000." Your customer says "$10,000." You then say, "Why don't we split the difference, and make it $10,500."

Once the final terms have been agreed upon and the deal has been closed, there will be some type of closing ceremony. This will differ depending on the type of negotiation. Sometimes it is merely a handshake. However, most of the time it consists of contracts being signed. When the contract is signed, the negotiation is closed. But, your work is not finished. It is important to recognize and thank your counterparty.

Most importantly, once the deal is signed, stand by your word.

If you want to have any credibility in the car business, you must stand by what you promised during any negotiation. This is true for everyone, but especially for wholesalers who hope to be dealing with the same customers on a routine basis. If you want your customer to trust you in the future, you must stand behind your word and your vehicles, in the present moment. In other words, if you described the car as having new brakes and new tires, make sure it has new brakes and new tires. To maintain credibility in the used car business it is important to honor all of the commitments you made during any negotiation process, even after the deal has been closed.

Things to keep in mind about Negotiation

- Negotiation is a major aspect of the used car business.
- Competitive or cooperative, choose which personal style fits you best.
- Preparation is the key to a successful negotiation.
- Being prepared means asking questions.
- Write your negotiation goals down.
- Focus on your goal.
- Remember the power of anchoring.
- When exchanging information, communication and listening skills are imperative.
- Follow up, once the deal is closed.
- Honor your commitments once the deal has closed.

Section IV

WHOLESALING

Wholesalers

In my biased opinion, wholesalers are the most underappreciated yet important part of the used car industry. Wholesalers provide much needed liquidity to the used car market and are often responsible for producing as many car deals as retail franchises. Most wholesalers are top notch car buyers and excellent business people. Wholesaling can be one of the most challenging and highest paying professions in the car business. But, it can also be the most stressful and lowest paying position in the car business.

Being a successful wholesaler means having a broad skill base. Wholesalers wear many different hats throughout the day. Because wholesale operations have fewer employees, it is more important for wholesalers to be knowledgeable in several aspects of the car industry. You will need to be part: market researcher, salesman, negotiator, purchasing agent, title clerk, and logistical guru.

- A good wholesaler knows how to do market research.
- A good wholesaler travels to find the bargains.
- A good wholesaler knows how to get retail deals.
- A good wholesaler knows the importance of relationships and negotiates accordingly.
- A good wholesaler is a logistical guru.

A good wholesaler knows how to do market research.

The goal of any market research initiative is to develop a deeper understanding of what your customers want to buy. Buying vehicles that are in demand is important for all car dealerships, but buying high demand vehicles is even more critical for wholesalers. Cars are always depreciating and any amount of time will cut into your profit margin. Since wholesalers operate with slimmer margins, time is always critical.

Most wholesalers have a core group of customers or dealerships they service. It is imperative to determine which vehicles are needed and wanted at these dealerships. *Your main job as a wholesaler is to determine which vehicles your customer wants and how much they will pay for those vehicles.* However, some UCMs are not always so open with their wholesalers about the type of vehicles they need. This may be because the UCM doesn't know which vehicle he needs to purchase or it may be because the UCM is very tight-lipped about this kind of information.

In either case, your goal is to extract as much information from the UCM or used car buyer as possible. You may only get general information, such as, "I need imports that don't have too many miles that I can sell around $12,000." Still, any amount of information you receive will help you perform your job better. As a wholesaler, you don't need to determine which types of vehicles the entire car driving population will want to buy. You only need to determine what types of vehicles your specific customers want to buy.

A good wholesaler travels to find the bargains.

A wholesaler's job is to buy vehicles that can be sold quickly for a profit. The bigger the profit is, the better. Unfortunately, as wholesalers, our margins are constantly getting squeezed. One way to combat margin contraction is to purchase vehicles outside of your home market. This means travelling to out-of-town auctions.

There are bargains to be found outside of your home territory. This is due to the fact that each car market in the United States is unique and different. For example, convertibles are much cheaper in Michigan during the winter months than they are in Florida. You can exploit these regional differences to your advantage.

I have found that the best auctions to attend are far away from your home market, but not too far. The auction has to be far enough away that pricing fluctuations can occur, but not so far that transportation costs become too large.

If you are having a difficult time sourcing desirable inventory at a good price, try attending a few auctions outside of your normal market area.

A good wholesaler knows how to get retail deals.

Retail deals are an excellent way to increase your monthly income. As a wholesaler, I viewed retail deals as strictly bonuses. I never counted on them, but I was happy when I got them. As a wholesaler, you can use your position and your low overhead to your advantage when pursuing retail customers.

The biggest asset a wholesaler has when competing against any large retail operation is low overhead. Because of this, price should be your major selling point. In other words, as a wholesaler, you have fewer expenses, so you can price your cars cheaper than your competition.

As a wholesaler, I would advertise the vehicles I was attempting to retail through Autotrader.com. For every make and model that I tried to retail, I wanted to be the price leader. I wanted to have the lowest price in town. This strategy didn't always result in a sale, but it did drive a significant amount of retail phone traffic to me. In other words, having the lowest price in town meant my phone was constantly ringing. Autotrader.com attracts an enormous number of shoppers, leveraging their online platform and tools meant that I could reach a large number of customers in a way that was simple and extremely cost effective.

I would post my vehicles on Autotrader.com as soon as they were purchased. I would price them for $1000 over the costs I had in the vehicle. This usually made me one of the cheapest options in town, which resulted in many retail deals. Being a wholesaler, my main objective was always to wholesale any vehicle I purchased as quickly as possible. Because of this, I was always receiving calls from customers about cars I no longer had in stock. However, this usually provided me an excellent opportunity to explain to a retail customer what services I could provide for them as a wholesaler.

I would describe the differences between retail facilities and wholesalers. I would explain to the potential customer that the cars I buy usually don't stay in my possession for very long. I would also explain to them the difference in expenses when buying a car from a retail dealership or from a wholesale operation that can also retail cars. Most of the time, this thorough explanation would earn a customer's trust and resulted in several retail car deals.

I further increased my retail business as soon as I started telling potential customers exactly how I priced my vehicles. My speech or "sales pitch" was honest and always the same. I would tell people, "Once I buy a vehicle, I will have a certain number of fees associated with it. The fees are usually very small, maybe an auction fee of $200-$300. Your price will be $1000 (sometimes $500 for friends) more than the total amount of fees I have in the car. The $1000 covers the liability I assume when I purchase any vehicle. It also includes the use of my dealer license, my dealer insurance, and my extensive experience that comes from purchasing several thousand vehicles during the course of a lifetime. $1,000, that's the price. Take it or leave it."

Most people took the deal. Most customers loved this idea. They thought it was simple and straight forward. I even offered to show them my expenses and invoices if they asked. But, no one ever asked. This kind of arrangement was convenient for me and it did not take time away from my wholesale operation. Remember, I only used retail deals to supplement my wholesale business. My average wholesale margin was between $400 and $500. I viewed my retail deals simply as wholesale deals with bigger margins.

I offered a very bare bones type of retail service. I did not offer any financing or warranty options. I only offered an inexpensive price. I would make suggestions about companies a customer could visit and receive financing or a warranty, but for the most part, I did very little hand holding with my customers.

One final note about retailing used cars. Always check the laws in your particular state. Each state has a different set of laws about what is considered retail, who can retail a vehicle, and how those retail services can be advertised. Before you start retailing vehicles, make sure that you are in compliance with your state's regulations.

A good wholesaler knows the importance of relationships and negotiates accordingly.

As a wholesaler, you should view the relationships you have with UCMs as marathons not sprints. You should also strive to gain as many profitable customer relationships as possible. The more customers you are working with, the more opportunities you will have to make deals happen. A busy wholesale operation can sell as many cars as a large franchise dealership, and they can do this with only having a few customers. Because of this customer dynamic, a wholesaler should have a negotiating style that is more consistent with a compromiser, rather than a competitor. Furthermore, because most wholesalers want to build long lasting relationships with dealerships, it might even be necessary and recommended to "lose" a few negotiations. In other words, you might need to take a loss on a few vehicles if it strengthens a profitable relationship with a dealership.

When I was a wholesaler, my biggest customers were import franchises (mainly Honda and Toyota) dealerships. In order to increase my volume, I was always on the lookout for more of these types of dealerships. I found that the easiest way to open a new business relationship with any UCM was to bring him a high demand vehicle at an extremely low price, even if that meant taking a loss on the vehicle. In the long run, the loss would be made up by having access to an additional dealership's inventory. As a wholesaler, having several diverse customers is imperative if you want to increase the number of cars you can buy and sell.

As a wholesaler, it seems that we should want to keep all of our customers. But, not all relationships are profitable. Some relationships take too much of our time and resources and don't provide an adequate amount of profit. Sometimes these relationships can exist with dealerships where you have had a long history. In these kind of situations, although it is difficult, it is often better to stop doing business with such a customer. As a wholesaler, it is more important to have a few excellent customers rather than many lackluster customers.

A good wholesaler is a logistical guru.

Because wholesalers are constantly transporting vehicles from one location to another, logistics is a major part of any wholesale operation. Cars need to be moved from the auction to dealerships and from dealerships to the auction. They need to be moved from dealership to dealership. Sometimes, they need to be reconditioned before they are sold and moved anywhere. There is also a title and a payment route that corresponds to each vehicle you wholesale. In other words, there are several logistical issues that must be addressed every day.

There are three basic methods for transporting vehicles:

- Lease or purchase your own tow truck and truck the vehicles yourself.
- Hire a 3rd party trucking service.
- Hire drivers.

I do not recommend leasing or purchasing your own truck. You are a wholesaler, not a truck driver. If you want to be a truck driver, then be a truck driver. If you want to be a wholesaler, spend your valuable time buying and selling used vehicles, not trucking them. Also, by performing the tow services yourself, you will add significant liabilities and costs to your overhead.

Using a 3rd party tow service has several benefits. First of all, someone else does all of the transporting, freeing up your valuable time. Further, your vehicles will be insured through the transportation company's insurance. It should be mentioned that before you decide to use ANY tow service, always verify their insurance coverage.

I mainly used trucking companies when transporting vehicles back from the auction because I travelled out of town to purchase most of my inventory. However, I prefer to use full time and part time drivers when moving vehicles locally. The reason for this is simple. You are not just delivering a vehicle, as a wholesaler, you are also: reconditioning the vehicle, delivering the title, receiving the check, and depositing the check in the bank.

Every wholesaler's goal is to get the money in the bank as soon as possible. A driver can expedite these processes because they perform other functions besides merely transporting a car. In other words, drivers can be extremely valuable in exchanging titles and checks, thus helping you get your money in the bank quicker and enabling you to better leverage your money.

A person who is responsible enough to deliver vehicles and perform title running functions is difficult to find. Even after you find and hire them, they typically require a lot of training and day-to-day management at first. However, once they are properly trained and motivated, they will be an invaluable resource for any wholesaler. A trained driver and title runner will free up more of your valuable time, allowing you to spend more time performing the activities that produce revenue for your company.

A tiny bit about the Used Car Business

Cell Phone Use

"I drive with my knees. Otherwise, how can I put on my lipstick and talk on my phone?" **Sharon Stone**

Because of the nature of our business, car people spend a lot of time talking on the telephone. It is what we do. We also tend to spend a lot of time in cars. This combination leads to a lot of talking on the phone while driving a car. Unfortunately for us, this is not the safest activity.

Countless statistics have shown that driving while distracted is the number one cause of traffic accidents in this country. Yet, we still drive while being distracted. According to national statistics on automobile accidents:

- A person dies in a car accident every 12 minutes.
- Each year, car crashes kill 40,000 people in the United States.
- The leading cause of death for individuals between 2 and 34 years old is motor vehicle crashes.
- Someone is injured by a car crash every 14 seconds and about two million of the people injured in car accidents each year suffer permanent injuries.[iv]

How many times have you been driving while talking on the phone and thumbing through a Black Book or NADA Guide? How many times have you done that today? I've done it. I have done it countless times. I knew it was unsafe at the time, yet I still did it. I eventually stopped when one of my close associates was involved in a serious automobile accident which was partially due to being distracted.

If you are a UCM or wholesaler who is constantly driving while being distracted, please stop now. There is no car deal that is worth getting in an accident. There is no telephone call that is worth getting in an accident. Your life and the life of others are worth more than that. Even if you are a wonderful driver, they are called accidents for a reason, and any amount of distraction while behind the wheel can lead to an accident.

If you do get an important call while driving, simply pull over in a safe place or politely tell the person that you will call them back soon. You will be safer, and you will be able to organize your thoughts better.

Many states are now implementing a law that requires the use of a hands free device while driving. Early adopters include New York and California. Do yourself a favor, buy a hands free device and use it.

No call or car deal is worth risking your life or the life of others.

Should you start your own wholesale company or work for someone else?

Running a wholesale business requires a considerable amount of capital. Exactly how much capital varies depending on how much experience you have as a wholesaler. It also depends on what kind of wholesaler you want to be.

There are three main types of wholesalers:

- The swapper.
- The reconditioning expert.
- The auction wholesaler.

The swapper uses other people's inventory instead of his own. Because many dealerships have strict inventory turn requirements, there will always be a demand for wholesalers who can: buy, sell, and swap vehicles. Often, a UCM will have a wholesaler perform many of these functions for a dealership. In these cases, the wholesaler is paid a flat fee for their services. This type of wholesaling requires very little capital.

The reconditioning expert is the type of wholesaler who makes money by being an expert at the value added service of reconditioning. These people usually purchase vehicles that need major reconditioning work. They then repair the vehicle and hope they can sell it for a profit. This type of wholesaling requires a significant amount of capital, both cash and floorplans. Paying for reconditioning work often requires a significant amount of cash. It will also place stress on your floorplan arrangements because reconditioning work will increase how long you are holding a car.

The auction wholesaler uses the auctions to purchase and sell inventory. This type of wholesaling also requires a substantial amount of capital. When buying and selling at auctions, you will have fees and expenses requiring cash. Your floorplan will also be stressed when using the auctions.

If you are new to wholesaling, I highly recommend going to work with a person who is currently making their living by wholesaling cars. Good wholesalers that are doing a large volume are very busy people. They are also always looking for quality help. They are always looking for a qualified driver or a title runner. This is probably one of the best ways to "learn the ropes." Working for another wholesaler will also give you the opportunity to expand your network of dealership contacts.

It takes several years as a wholesaler to develop a solid financial history. It takes time to build a banking history. It takes time to get your auction floorplan established to the point where you can source several cars. It takes time for your bank to familiarize themselves with the enormous amount of transactions that will be processed through your account. This does not happen overnight, it is a gradual process. Working for an established wholesale operation will give you access to a larger money supply. This is one of the major reasons to work for someone else.

I do not recommend going on your own as a wholesaler until you have: an established financial history, an extensive network of contacts, and a considerable amount of experience buying and selling used cars. These factors will help you make wholesaling a profitable and an exciting career.

The people you meet in the Used Car Business

Let YOUR VOICE Be Heard

The used car business can be very frustrating at times. We have all experienced difficult days, and there will be more challenging days in the future. Times are rarely easy for the used car professional, but recently, life has been exceptionally difficult. Most economists have stated that the current business climate is the toughest since the Great Depression. Yet, the used car professional continues to demonstrate their ability to adapt.

There are thousands of people throughout this country who earn their living through the used car industry. For many of those people, recent times have been disastrous. Although the used car industry often gets stereotyped by the public, we are in fact, all individuals. We are all different. We have different backgrounds, different jobs, different family structures, different talents, and different desires. In many ways, we are also very similar. The people that comprise the Used Car Industry are:

- Used car managers
- Used car salespeople
- Wholesalers
- Auctioneers, ring men, auction title personnel, etc...
- Truckers
- Mechanics
- Porters

- Employees of: BlackBook, Kelley Blue Book, NADA Guides, etc...
- Employees of Autotrader.com, Dealer.com, Cars.com, etc...
- Detailers, window repair technicians, interior repairmen, wheel repairmen, lot washers, etc...
- Employees of Reynolds & Reynolds, ADP, etc...

And the list goes on and on.

I said in the first chapter of this book that if I was forced to choose my favorite thing about the used car business, it would be the people. Everyone in the used car industry works hard and works long hours. We also have very similar experiences within our job functions. In other words, a Porter for a Chevy store in Arkansas has roughly the same day-to-day experiences as a Porter for a Honda dealership in Florida. A UCM in a large city in California has roughly the same job duties as a UCM in a small town in Maine. The people are different, the stores may be different, but the job remains the same.

What does this similarity mean for each of us? It means that we all have the ability to help others in our industry by sharing our own experiences. Not only **can** we help others, we **should** help others. It might be a small business tip or a funny story from one UCM that keeps another UCM from having a melt-down during a bad day at the dealership. It might be your words that help another person. Please tell us your stories. Visit www.UsedCarVoice.com and share some of your favorite experiences from your career in the used car industry.

The last few years have been difficult for many Used Car Professionals, but they have been more difficult for many others in our country. Most notably are the American soldiers that return home from war with a life changing injury. For these people, life will never be the same. For many of them, tasks that were once easy to perform are now impossible to manage. The Disabled American Veterans (DAV) has been helping wounded American Soldiers in this country since 1920. However, their mission has never been more critical than it currently is.

I never thought I would have the: desire, time, energy, or patience to write a book about anything. Several months ago, I happened to watch a webcast about individuals who write and publish books in order to donate money to their favorite causes or organizations. I immediately thought of the DAV. Further, I knew that American Used Car Professionals are generous and good hearted people. Yes, some are snakes in the grass, but the majority are good people. My hope was that I could write something that would be informative and entertaining that would help people in the used car business make more money and therefore be able to donate money to the Disabled American Veterans. It is that thought that kept me going throughout this book writing process.

For every copy of this book that is sold, a donation of $1 will be made to the Disabled American Veterans (DAV) Charitable Service Trust.

If you enjoyed this book, tell others in the used car profession about this book. Tell your UCM or tell your wholesalers, tell people you interact with at the auctions. Word of mouth advertising is very powerful and can spread very quickly. One Dollar does not sound like much, but if the thousands of people in the used car industry pull together; our industry really can make a difference. See, I told you I always ask for the referral at the end.

For more information on the DAV and the DAV service trust please visit www.DAV.org.

For more about the Used Car Industry and to share YOUR thoughts and experiences please visit www.UsedCarVoice.com.

Good Luck and I wish you Happy Selling.

Appendix 1

Survey questions

Used Car Managers and Buyers

What is the most important aspect of managing a used car inventory?

Name one mistake that cost you money, which you have corrected.

What was the worst (biggest loss, biggest headache, etc) vehicle you ever bought?

What is the most important aspect of employee management?

If you could change one thing about your dealership, what would it be?

Which department in your dealership is the weakest? Why?

What attributes make a successful used car manager?

What attributes make a successful used car buyer?

What is your favorite auction food?

Do you have a humorous story about a customer experience that you would like to share?

Do you have a humorous story about another used car professional that you would like to share?

Please feel free to visit www.UsedCarVoice.com to provide **your** answers to these survey questions.

Used Car Salespeople

What is the most important part of selling used cars?

Name one mistake you used to do, that you have corrected.

What attributes make a successful used car salesperson?

Do you have a story about a "challenging" customer interaction?

Do you have a story about a "successful" customer interaction?

Appendix 2

Books to read

Here is a list of excellent, thought-provoking books that will help you improve your business abilities.

Negotiation

Bargaining for advantage- G. Richard Shell

The power of nice- Robert M Shapiro

Management

The seven habits of highly effective people- Stephen R Covey

How to win friends and influence people- Dale Carnegie

The art of war- Sun Tzu

Management- Peter F. Drucker

The E myth revisited- Michael Gerber

One minute manager- Kenneth H. Blanchard and Spencer Johnson

First, break all the rules: what the world's greatest managers do differently- Marcus Buckingham and Curt Coffman

Sales

The greatest salesman in the world- OG Mandino

Spin selling- Neil Rakham

The little red book of selling- Jeffrey Gitomer

Attitude 101- John C Maxwell

General Business

The tipping point- Malcolm Gladwell

The richest man in Babylon- George S Clason

The automatic millionaire- David Bach

Sam Walton, made in America- Sam Walton and John Huey

Notes

---

[i] United States Department of Labor, http://www.bls.gov, 2009.

[ii] G. Richard Shell. Bargaining for Advantage. New York: Penguin Books, 2000.

[iii] G. Richard Shell. Bargaining for Advantage. New York: Penguin Books, 2000.

[iv] http://www.nhtsa.dot.gov

Made in the USA
Charleston, SC
13 May 2011